URBAN MYTHS

URBAN MYTHS

Andreas Markides

Troubador Publishing Ltd
Unit E2 Airfield Business Park,
Harrison Road, Market Harborough,
Leicestershire. LE16 7UL
Tel: 0116 2792299
Email: books@troubador.co.uk
Web: www.troubador.co.uk

ISBN 978 1805145 073

British Library Cataloguing in Publication Data.
A catalogue record for this book is available from the British Library.

Typeset in 11pt Minion Pro by Troubador Publishing Ltd, Leicester, UK

This, my first book in English, is dedicated to Asclepius.

CONTENTS

I have worked for nearly forty years in the built environment profession. As a transport planner and an engineer, I have enjoyed working with many other affiliated disciplines such as architects, planners, developers, project managers and urban designers. I have made many friends along the way and together we have faced, and grappled with, many challenges. It has struck me that most of these challenges were not necessarily of a *technical* nature (those were the easy ones). The most difficult challenges have actually been those relating to human interaction – how people work together, how they respond to adversity, what priorities each person attaches to different issues and so on.

In fact, human behaviour takes me closer to my other interest (or should I say passion) in life, which is classical Greek civilisation and Greek myths. From a young age I have been fascinated by all the stories about Pegasus, the beautiful horse that could fly; Odysseus's ten-year-long return journey from Troy; Oedipus's inability to avoid his tragic fate of killing his father and marrying his mother; various monsters such as the Minotaur, Medusa and the Hydra; and the philosopher Socrates who had pronounced that, "I know one thing, and that is that I know nothing"! All this has made me realise that, as the author Charlotte

Higgins famously said, "the Greek myths are the opposite of timeless; they are timely".

Two years ago, I decided to try and bring my two interests together and I therefore started writing short articles that brought Greek myths and the built environment profession together. On the face of it, this seemed incongruous, but I asked myself the question: do any of the stories from ancient Greece have any relevance to the built environment discipline and more generally to modern-day life? I was astounded to realise that there are a huge number of similarities and that the stories from thousands of years ago still resonate today. Greed, the pursuit of happiness, hubris, our relationship to nature, the way we work, the way we build cities, the way we conduct our lives – all of these themes are eternal.

I have now put together twenty-two such articles. Some of them have already appeared in the journal of the Academy of Urbanism *Here and Now*. The response to the stories in the journal has been positive and this has encouraged me to put all the articles together into this collection. Sprinkled amongst these articles you will also find a couple of my poems, as writing poetry has also been one of my secret and lifelong pleasures.

I am grateful to my wife Kay and my four children Helen, Nicki, Steph and Alex who have patiently endured being my guinea pigs whilst at the same time being my sternest critics (I know they meant well)! Huge thanks also to some special friends (particularly Dan Bone, Professor Costas Markides and Andrew Swift) who have similarly offered some valuable comments. A special thank you to

David Rudlin whose illustrations have vastly enriched my collection.

I hope that you will enjoy the stories in the same way that people enjoy a well-built place!

Andreas
2024

A FEW WORDS BY SIMON RICKETTS

I have always loved working alongside Andreas on development projects. Some of us can lose our sense of humanity, of what drives all of us beneath the surface, of what makes us tick – caught up in the technical and financial challenges of what is on our desk or screen. But not Andreas.

In fact, I have been too slow to realise that what interests Andreas about transportation planning isn't the cars, or the trains, or the buses or the cycles. It's the drivers, the passengers, the riders – the people. What interests Andreas about clients is them as people. And what interests Andreas about the businesses he has successfully led is again the people within them.

Andreas's pride for his Cypriot heritage (second only to his pride for his family, I suspect) has always been plain to see. But it was still a surprise to me when these wonderful vignettes started to appear on LinkedIn, explaining individual Greek (and other) myths by reference to the modern world around us. And what a perfect use of modern social media to breathe life into these old stories with their timeless messages.

Our challenges seem uniquely of our time: how to combat climate change, how to harness artificial intelligence, how to breathe new uses into our town centres and find decent homes for those who need them. Andreas's stories help in a gentle way by reminding us how others have articulated the challenges and the pitfalls. Some of them will be well known, if hidden by the clatter of day-to-day life; others unknown – beautiful allegories to be discovered, derivations finally understood for modern-day expressions we use without thinking.

Classicism and a knowledge of the past should not be regarded as elitist or in some way an unnecessary luxury or irrelevance. I hope you all enjoy, and perhaps marvel slightly at, these twenty-two labours of Markides.

Simon Ricketts
April 2023
Partner
Town Legal LLP
www.townlegal.com
Most highly rated planning law team in the country (*Planning Magazine* annual Planning Law Survey 2019, 2020, 2021 & 2022).

For over twenty-five years I have enjoyed and benefitted massively from Andreas's personal approach to transport planning. We have worked on many projects together, of which we are both proud.

As a transport engineer, he is expected to work with numbers, data and facts and be able to demonstrate compliance with models, traffic counts and not increase the length of traffic jams! He has had an extremely successful career in doing this, but I have always seen him bring something different for a transport expert: a human perspective. He brings humility and a sense of what is best. What is best not for cars but for people and the places they inhabit. He is a people person.

So, it is inspiring and refreshing to read the twenty-two essays that bring together Andreas's passion for people and places with Greek mythology. Greek mythology captures stories concerning the gods, heroes and rituals of ancient Greeks which has had a significant influence on Western civilisation. In the essays, Andreas brings perspective and insight in his observations to the modern world and the relevance to those ancient scriptures. His words express what we can all see, and what is wrong with the way we live our lives. In all his essays, he endeavours to answer the question 'what can we learn?' from these accounts from many centuries ago.

For Plato, he wanted to define the 'perfect place' where people would 'be able to carry their prosperity with moderation'. In today's world of excess, of obscene personal wealth and huge disparity between the rich and the poor, Andreas observes the threats to this moderation, and its impact on people and the planet. In the essays we also learn about the effects of law and governance. I know how Andreas has adopted these beliefs through fairness and equality applied in the businesses that he has run.

For me, Andreas has reminded us how the words of ancient Greece remain as relevant today as the day they were written. Those timeless principles of what makes a civilised and responsible society where the quality of people's lives is foremost.

Marcus Adams
April 2023
Managing Partner
JTP
www.jtp.co.uk
Winner of over 250 awards including Best Companies' 100 Best Mid-Sized Companies to Work for 2021 and AJ and Building Design Employer of the Year.

EVERYTHING FLOWS

Many years ago, when I was still in school, I was told about an ancient Greek philosopher called Heraclitus who lived in Ephesus on the coast of Asia Minor. This philosopher is little known today, but he is still remembered because of the following two words that he uttered: "everything flows". He explained his statement by referring to a river and went on to say that "no river is ever the same, as it is constantly flowing and constantly changing". He concluded that the same is true about so much else in life.

I have often reflected on this statement and wondered of its significance and possible application to my own life. In particular, did it have any relevance to my own profession of traffic engineering and to the wider field of planning? At first, I thought that the statement held no particular significance, but more and more, as I reflect about my near forty years in this profession, I realise that Heraclitus may have been spot on.

For example, I have watched with much fascination (and no little bemusement) how demand for different land uses changes over time. So, in the '80s, a lot of us were building something which came to be known as a 'business park'. No longer were we satisfied with industrial estates as those were ugly and outdated. The Americans were teaching us that we needed to build business premises 'in the park'. Once we had satisfied our insatiable appetite with that particular import, we turned our attention and energies to another – that of the multiplex cinema. Subsequently we moved to offices – each building boasting to be better (architecturally and in locational terms) than the one before it. I can still remember the fuss that was made about Ralph Erskine's Ark building which was located so that it would become the western gateway into London (even though in the end it had priced itself too highly with the result that no tenant could be found for some time). And so, we arrive at the present day, which is all about housing and yet more housing.

Nothing exemplifies better our changing approach to land-use planning than our policies towards retail development. Remember the big push in the '80s for supermarkets and then hypermarkets? These huge, monolithic structures were springing up everywhere (along with their associated sea of car parking). Then suddenly a voice had the courage to point out that this trend was actually killing off our high streets. There was tremendous opposition to this questioning of the 'retail model', and I can still remember how vociferously the main operators used every possible argument to stop any change on the grounds that they could operate only if they were allowed to have traditionally large stores, surrounded by car parking, on the edge of different settlements. But change we did and, perhaps amazingly, we now have a Tesco Express and a Sainsbury's Local on every high street and at most railway stations – and there are no car parks in sight! Amazingly still, the bread that these smaller stores sell smells as delicious as that which, a few years ago, you could only have bought from their supermarkets.

This change has now resulted in retailers such as IKEA reviewing their traditional way of operating. One of the most startling manifestations of this change is the new IKEA store which has been proposed in the middle of Vienna; this store will provide no parking spaces at all! There is no possibility anymore of loading up your car with their goods – even though you could carry them on public transport, if you wished. As an added bonus, the store will be a green building and there will also be public access to its roof terrace, offering stunning views of the city.

In my own profession of traffic engineering, we have seen one of the biggest changes in approach and policy. Up until the late '80s, traffic engineers would do everything possible in order to increase traffic capacities and keep traffic flowing smoothly. Then suddenly another lone voice had the temerity to inform us that "the more roads we build, the more traffic will be created". It was a little like the Hydra – you chop one head off and two more spring forth! This prompted a lot of soul searching amongst traffic engineers who were momentarily stunned and confused. What were they supposed to do? Provide traffic capacity or hinder it?

This perplexity has continued to the present day when the concepts of sustainability and healthy living arrived to put a last nail in the coffins of trip generation and road building. Traffic engineers now know that, far more important than traffic capacity, is the provision of quality spaces, more human streets and places which contribute to healthier, happier communities.

Alongside the treatment of traffic, we have also been changing our approach to parking provision. I remember distinctly that in the late '80s and well into the '90s, all my clients (whether these were developers, house builders or institutions such as hospitals or universities) would not only demand from me but expect that I would make the strongest possible case for the provision of the maximum number of parking spaces. That message started to become diluted with John Prescott's sustainability agenda in the late '90s with the result that, nowadays, a lot of my clients will ask that we make as little provision for parking as possible. The premise is that reduced parking means more land for either landscaping or more development. It just so happens that reduced parking could also mean more sustainable developments, but the fact remains that not only has our position changed but we have actually gone full circle from wanting the most to wanting the least!

Coming back to Heraclitus, it is indisputable that in my narrow field of traffic engineering, as well as in the wider field of planning, there is constant change; the river is flowing. However, if everything is constantly changing, does this mean that we are always wrong?

We were wrong in the '60s when we were building what are now regarded to be awful and unsafe residential towers. We were also wrong when, subsequently, we started to build what we now consider to be soulless housing estates. Are we perhaps wrong even now when we are embarking (despite much questioning and cynicism) on a path towards a more sustainable world?

The answer is *no*; I do not think so. Heraclitus is correct up to a point. We and the world around us change constantly until no more change can be afforded. A volcano will continue to spew out lava and change in its form and intensity until it dies. A tree will constantly change (green leaves in the spring, brown in the autumn, etc.) until its trunk is eaten by a fungus and it falls to the ground dead. A river will continue to flow until it dries up. The same with humans; we will have reached our end-state and will certainly die if we fail to adopt a more sustainable way of life.

We are currently entering what can be described as our 'sustainable period' (in planning as well as in every other human activity). We are but a second away from the end-state. We simply *must* wholeheartedly embrace and adopt everything that this idea entails. If we lost heart and changed again it would probably mean the end of the world as we know it. Certainly, the signs are ominous, in terms of our natural environment as well as our own physical and mental health. We simply *must* try to create better, healthier and more sustainable communities. This is the final stage of our evolution in both planning and traffic engineering. We cannot afford to change anymore!

In conclusion, Heraclitus was mostly correct – everything changes until we reach the end-state, at which point we have no other options. We must persevere on the path that protects our environment, provides for healthier living and creates quality places. If nothing else, even at this eleventh hour and 2,500 years after Heraclitus's proclamation, we will have proved him wrong!

HAPPINESS

At several of my presentations in the last few years I have spoken about how good design and better places (however that term may be defined) give rise to happier people. Often, I have then made the bold statement that happy people usually go on to "create civilisations" – and at this point I have referenced back to classical Athens with its invigorating agora, its bustling harbour and magnificent temples.

I have then contrasted that picture with modern-day Athens: its congested, traffic-choked streets, its *nefos* (the dark cloud that hovers over Athens on many hot days and makes breathing difficult), the beggars on the streets... I have exemplified this degradation by showing a picture of one of many riots that took place in Athens during the country's economic collapse. The point I was making was that happy people feel confident about themselves, and this leads to creativity. In contrast, unhappy/angry people have no time to create; instead, they just destroy.

What I find surprising is that I have never been challenged by any member of the audience about this presumption! I took that to mean that (intuitively at least) all of us agree that better places create happier people.

Using that as my platform, I now go on to ask myself the bigger question of what is happiness, and how can it be achieved? A better physical environment certainly helps, but is that all that is required? The answer of course is *no* – much more is needed, such as good health, friendships, love and enjoying the respect of others.

All this is exemplified by the following story from Herodotus: there lived in Athens a wise man called Solon; he is the one who laid the foundations for Athens to acquire its set of laws which eventually led to a democratic system. Solon's reputation spread far and wide amongst the then known world and at one point he was invited to the palace of King Croesus of Lydia who was known for his enormous wealth. Croesus showed Solon round his stunning palace and all his treasures; at the end of the tour, he asked Solon if he could name a happier man than King Croesus. Solon surprised his host by naming an unknown Athenian named Tellus. Solon explained that this man had fought bravely for his country and that he was fortunate enough to see his children and grandchildren before he died in old age. Undaunted, Croesus went on to question who the *second* happiest person was, and Solon replied that it was probably two young men from Argos who were known for their love and respect for their mother. They too had died peacefully in the temple where their mother had been a priestess.

Croesus was very angry with these responses and asked Solon why his own happiness had been dismissed as less worthy than those of a few ordinary men. Solon went on to explain that in the length of a lifetime there is much that one does not wish to experience. Consequently, a human life cannot be judged happy until it has been completed. Even a rich king, seemingly blessed with happiness now, may at any time in the future meet with disasters which will invalidate his apparent happiness.

Croesus called Solon a fool and threw him out of the palace. Soon afterwards, King Cyrus of Persia invaded Croesus's kingdom; Cyrus was triumphant, and Croesus himself was captured and ordered to be executed. As Croesus was about to be burned on a pyre, he cried out Solon's name. At that point, Cyrus ordered for the pyre to be stopped because he was curious to find out what Croesus meant by calling out "Solon, Solon – how right you were!". Croesus then related his encounter with Solon, and Cyrus was so moved that he ordered Croesus to be freed.

So, happiness is many things, but it is mostly transient. It is only once we have seen someone's *entire* life (and importantly the manner of his/her death) that we will be able to judge if they have had a happy life. There are of course many cases that prove Solon right. The almighty emperor Nero committed suicide at age thirty. Julius Caesar – who, moments earlier, had attained a status as close to a deity as is possible – lay dead in the Senate with more than twenty Roman daggers stuck into him. And in modern times one can name President Ceausescu of Romania who was shot together with his wife by his own countrymen as they were trying to flee the country. The almighty Idi Amin fled his own country and died a fugitive and alone in Saudi Arabia. Pinochet of Chile became an international parasite. The Shah of Iran, who at one point thought of himself as supreme emperor, ended up unable to find a country that would accept him, even to treat his cancer.

Outside politics we have Jeffrey Epstein with his several mansions, who ended up hanging himself in prison. The Hollywood mogul Harvey Weinstein, who is now rotting in prison, and so on…

Despite the power and riches that they had once enjoyed, can any of these people be judged to have had a happy life?

Final word on this must be given to Socrates who believed that only people with self-knowledge could find true happiness. According to Socrates, happiness does not flow from physical or external conditions such as bodily pleasures, wealth or power. Happiness arises only from living a 'good life'…

The big question of course is: what is a 'good life'? Again, Socrates (via the writings of Plato) provides the answer: happiness (or well-being) is the highest aim of moral thought and conduct.

And this brings me back to my original statement that the creation of better places leads to civilisations. How is that done? By freeing people of ugly thoughts and liberating the mind, thereby leading to 'moral thought and conduct'. That's what a good place does! And that's how we achieve happiness. At this point I should make clear that the creation of better places is not only about the physical environment that we live in. It is also about the *people* who live in and contribute to that environment; in other words, our community. A healthy and principled community living in a joyful place are the essential prerequisites for a happy life.

Isn't this what Pericles was referring to, in his famous funeral oration to the Athenians? He was telling his fellow countrymen "you should be very proud because you have managed to build such a wonderful city" – a *place* that fulfils you; that makes you happy. And 'creating civilisation' then becomes nothing but inevitable!

GREED

Just over a year ago, I was intrigued and a little shaken by the famous Westferry case. Some of you will remember it: in May 2020, the then Secretary of State for Housing, Communities and Local Government, Robert Jenrick, accepted that his approval of a £1 billion luxury housing development on Westferry Printworks on the Isle of Dogs, had been unlawful. The 1,500-home development was proposed by Richard Desmond, a Conservative Party donor. The government's planning inspector had previously advised against the scheme, as it delivered an inadequate amount of affordable housing and the height of the tower would have been detrimental to the character of the area. However, Jenrick approved the scheme on 14 January, knowing that an approval by that date would enable Richard Desmond to avoid having to pay the council's infrastructure levy of between £30 and £50 million (which could have been used instead to fund schools and medical facilities).

This rather infamous case made me ask myself the obvious question: why do some people place financial gain above all other considerations? Why do they always want more money? Is greed all-pervasive in our world?

Most curious of all are people who manage to reach a point in their lives when they have amassed enough wealth to enable them and their families to have a comfortable life, and yet they still want more! A prime example of this has been the ex-prime minister David Cameron. Nobody can dispute that Cameron (by virtue of his government pension, his own family's wealth, his wife's business, his fees from lectures, etc.) has a certain amount of financial comfort. And yet, he sought to become wealthier by associating himself with the 'toxic banker' Lex Greensill. Why? How much more comfortable would his life have become?

There are of course numerous similar stories, including the recent news item that the eighty-five or so hereditary peers have claimed half a million in expenses during the first six months of the pandemic. What exactly did these gentlemen and ladies do that justified claiming half a million from the taxpayer and, more importantly, did they have a need for this money?

All of these cases bring to mind the story of King Midas who, asked by a god to make one wish, said that he wanted everything that he touched to turn to gold. The first thing that he touched after being granted his wish, was his own young daughter, who had run to hug him in the morning! He then touched his plate of food… King Midas soon realised his folly and pleaded for forgiveness, but it would appear that his example has not taught *us* any lessons. We always want more! Why?

Staying within the confines of our own industry, it is worth asking the question: is the Westferry case unique, or is our own professional world afflicted by greed just like all other strands of life? The newspapers are full of stories about the massive payments made to chief executives of many national house builders. Then there was the recent report about the chief executives of the four biggest building companies linked to the Grenfell fire who have collectively received nearly £50 million in pay, bonuses, shares and dividends since the disaster. And finally, what about the densification of development and the promotion of high-rise living, particularly the exclusive apartments that are being offered to overseas sheikhs and oligarchs. Is this a correct practice, or is it merely greed by a few prospective developers and by the government itself?

I conclude that greed is all-pervasive in our world. The big question is: how can we eliminate greed and, in particular, why do people who, by any measure, should have enough, always want more? I personally have no answer to these questions, other than perhaps that this is the result of the capitalist system that we live in. Capitalism likes to reward success!

But is there a better system? Communism has failed resoundingly, and at the other extreme, dictatorships deliver wealth to dictators (and their small circle of associates), at the expense of the rest of the population.

We are therefore left with capitalism, but perhaps the best answer is capitalism with a little more morality? Thousands of years ago, Plato said that we would achieve the ideal state only if politicians became philosophers or if philosophers became politicians. Is there a politician in the world that would nowadays come anywhere close to being called a philosopher?

Despite the pessimism of all of the above examples, I remain positive, and I will finish with the following short story which provides a glimmer of hope that, for some people at least, more and more money is not the ultimate objective.

The story is about two American writers (Kurt Vonnegut and Joseph Heller). They had once been to a party hosted by a billionaire on Shelter Island, and the two of them had the following conversation:

Kurt: "Joe, how does it make you feel to know that our host only yesterday may have made more money than your novel *Catch-22* has earned in its entire history?"

Joe: "I've got something that he can never have."

Kurt: "What on earth could that be, Joe?"

Joe: "The knowledge that I have enough!"

REFUGEES

We are constantly bombarded with news about the fate of refugees and how one group of refugees is heading towards the island of Lampedusa, another is on the French coast plotting their way to England, whilst others may be languishing on the island of Lesbos.

This has prompted me to write about my own experience as a refugee from Cyprus. The story is probably well known, if rather old now…

In the summer of 1974, Turkey invaded Cyprus, which is where I was born. I was fifteen years old at the time and growing up in a small village of less than a thousand people. It was a very happy existence with two loving (if a little strict) parents, kids playing in the streets and an overpowering smell from the blossom of the orchards which constituted the livelihood of most families in the village.

For reasons that are not relevant here, Turkey invaded Cyprus that summer and after a short war (the small island of Cyprus stood no chance against a military power from NATO), Turkey

was able to capture about 40% of the northern part of the island. I still remember the fighting, that I watched from a distance, and I can still see vividly before my eyes the war planes dropping their napalm bombs on several villages and the line of Turkish troops advancing steadily and getting closer and closer to our village.

At one point my parents decided that, like many other people, we should abandon our home. All the family (two parents, five children under the age of fifteen and the inevitable black-clad grandmother) piled into my father's car and drove away to safety. We thought that this would have been for a short time, but we are yet to return to my ancestral home. In that instant, my parents lost everything they had: their home, their orchards and all their possessions, which have all been in the control of the Turkish army since then.

I have often wondered how I would have reacted if anything like that had ever befallen me and my own family. I admire the way that my parents responded. Even though they were overwhelmed with sadness and momentarily paralysed by their great loss, they never succumbed. I remember to this day when my father gathered all of us together and said in a firm tone: "We have lost everything, but I give you my word that all five of you will go on to study at a university." I do not know how they managed to do it, but my parents have kept that promise.

During the immediate aftermath of the invasion, I also remember standing in long queues to collect second-hand clothes, shoes and food that were distributed to all the refugees by the United Nations and various other agencies. And I vividly remember the rows and rows of tents that were swiftly set up in different (usually barren and unforgiving) locations, in order to house the refugees.

You might ask – what has been the effect of all this on yourself? I can honestly say that I consider this catastrophe to be a blessing! This may sound perverse, but it has taught me to be strong and to fight for better things (like my parents did). It has also taught me that, even though money is important, it is far less important than many other things – again, see how my parents were able to rebuild their lives even after they had lost everything. Finally, it has taught me the value of friendships (so many people stood by us during those awful times) and the importance of a kind word, particularly to people who are down; it can have an electrifying effect!

It is this last point that I would like to focus on because, since that fateful summer in 1974, there have been dozens and dozens more wars around the world, and these have had the inevitable consequence of people losing their homes, their land and, in many cases, their loved ones. We call all these people 'refugees', but none of us really appreciate the horrors that such people undergo for days, months and years.

We watch with empathy but helplessly (and with some indifference, as we go about our busy lives) all the new streams of refugees that are constantly invading our comfortable lives. Remember the pictures on the news of long lines of people fleeing their homes either on foot, tractors or battered-down cars, following the Yugoslav wars? Remember the war in Georgia or the catastrophic conflict in Afghanistan? Remember Eritrea, Libya and, more recently, Syria, Iraq, Myanmar, Armenia and the savage war in Ukraine? The grim litany is endless and knows how to constantly renew itself…

People's lives are utterly shattered by one conflict or another. In fact, looking back in history, it would seem that the world simply goes from one turbulence to the next – and each turbulence produces its own refugees. From biblical times when Moses and the Jews were fleeing Egypt to later times when the Irish and Italians went to America; the Greeks to Australia; Mexicans attempting to break down Donald Trump's wall. It is clear that, to a certain extent, we are all either refugees or their descendants!

And yet – and yet! There is always a wall between the refugees and us; it is always them and us. Very rarely do we welcome them with open arms. Nor do we for a moment recognise that, if these people were given the choice, they would much rather raise their families in their own homeland. Even all these years later, and despite a life which has now become comfortable, my parents would repeatedly say that their one remaining wish is for them to be buried in the humble cemetery of their small village. Time has regrettably taken that wish away from my mother now, but my father is still dreaming of that…

So, instead of seeing refugees as pests and invaders of our comfortable lives, we should embrace them. Only when we give them opportunities and treat them with kindness will refugees be able to fulfil their natural potential. At that point we will surely appreciate their worth as we will have seen how, in their different ways, they have enriched our own lives.

Kindness will comfort and inspire them, but will it heal their wounds? I have recently read in *The Times* newspaper about a young woman's tragedy in Mosul (Iraqi Kurdistan) and it reminded me once again that my own misfortune fifty years ago is nothing compared to the tragedies that are constantly experienced by countless people around the world. That woman's story starts with her two-year old daughter who had been killed by a sniper. The bullet then passed through the child's body into her husband, a 33-year old teacher who had been clasping the girl to his chest. He fell and also died two hours later in the debris of a garden, as a battle raged around them. In the morning she loaded her husband's body onto a wheelbarrow and pushed it through the ruins, looking for the cemetery. In the process she started bleeding as she had been six months pregnant and soon afterwards she lost her unborn child.

A single sniper's bullet killed all three members of this woman's family. What life has she now got left? And will she one day seek to get on a boat to escape the troubles in her homeland, hoping for a better life elsewhere? And will her heart be broken for ever or will she be able, at some point, to experience happiness and to stand tall?

And how will *we* answer her, when she knocks on our door?

KYRA

(This article first appeared in the Academy of Urbanism's journal under a specialist section called MY PLACE which is curated by John Mullin.)

I came to the UK more than forty years ago when I was sixteen. In that time, I have had a happy professional life, and I have built a beautiful family with my wife Kay. Our home is in Hampshire, and we both love it. And yet, the place that haunts me the most is a tiny village in Cyprus where I grew up. The village is called Kyra (*Geera* in the Cypriot dialect), and it had a population of less than a thousand people. Those people were mostly occupied with agriculture, cultivating different crops and vegetables on their land. In 1974, when Turkey invaded Cyprus, all of us fled the village in order to save ourselves from the bombing and the advancing troops. In an instant we became refugees – a term that tragically almost defines our world.

It has now been nearly fifty years since I was forced to leave everything in that village, and I can still smell the blossom of the trees in the orchards; I can hear the shouts of the kids playing football in the narrow streets; and I can see the beauty of the multicoloured wild flowers that spring from the arid earth after the first rainfall in the spring. I tried to reflect these memories in a short poem which I have shared below:

UPROOTED

The uninvited guests came,
and we hurriedly gathered some loose objects
from another life.

The jasmine at the entrance to the house,
as it blew gently in the evening breeze.
Battle-weary Teucer,[1]
disembarking from his ship at Salamis.
Our neighbour returning from his field,
on his tractor.

They were but a bundle of moments.
In no time, we packed them away.
Where did we pack them,
for we had no boxes?
And we carried them with us.
How were we able to carry them,
for we had no strength?

We are still carrying them,
silently and permanently,
in our heads.

---

1   *Teucer is a Homeric hero who established the first Greek
ettlement on Cyprus at a place called Salamis. You can still
see (and marvel at) this ancient city which is located on the
outskirts of Famagusta.*

This raises the obvious question: is a place something that we (architects, engineers and planners) create in a *physical* sense, or is it a multitude of moments that have shaped our lives?

TRANQUILITY

When I first came to England, some forty years ago, my English was very limited. I certainly did not know the meaning of the word 'commuter'. I now have a much better idea of that word's definition as I have been a commuter for many years.

On occasions during my trips into and out of London during this time, I would look at my fellow commuters in disbelief – they would be reading a paper, speaking to someone on the phone or simply snoozing, but there would always be an anxious look on their faces. That look would bring to my mind a hungry wolf, at the moment when he is finally and tiredly circling his prey. This would be the look of someone in constant search of something else – something more.

And at some point, the pack of wolves would attack its prey. That would be the moment when the train would arrive at its destination and pandemonium would ensue. The force would be unleashed and everyone would then be rushing in different directions, bumping into objects and people, eyes darting this way and that, many of them gasping for breath and anxiously searching – for what?

This journey would be but one part of life in London, one of the busiest cities in the world. Nothing ever stops in London; everything is constantly moving at a frantic pace. In fact, those who work in London try to outdo each other by how busy they are. It is almost a crime to admit that you are not busy. Everyone is always at meetings or on the phone, about one thing or other; always running but very rarely standing still. London is of course not an exception as we encounter similar frenetic behaviour in many other parts of the world.

Inevitably this leads me to ask the question: is this fast, tumultuous existence worth it? Has it provided us with a happier life than, let's say, fifty years ago when the tempo of life was a little slower? In my case I can hardly wait to flee London's rat race, in search of the tranquility of my home. It is clear that the professional path that I have chosen may have provided me with material gains, but it is doubtful if it has given me a peaceful life. Maybe I have used my education and subsequent career in the wrong way! Perhaps I should have put all the knowledge that I had acquired and all my energy into something else. Or maybe I should not have allowed my professional life to be so predominant. Maybe I should have given more of my time to other pursuits. I have read somewhere that nearly 50% of a Dutch person's time is dedicated to 'leisure' pursuits. That sounds a far more harmonious lifestyle.

In fact, isn't leisure time a lot more important than a busy professional life? Isn't the opportunity to pursue one's true interests (whether that's fishing or going to the theatre, reading a good book or enriching one's life with travel or dialogue with friends) what leads to a civilised society? In other words, should we not permit ourselves more time to be *creative*, rather than be confined to a prescribed professional existence in the hope that it will furnish us with comforts? I of course recognise the importance of a working life to the economy, but shouldn't the balance be away from a busy professional life and closer to leisure and creative pursuits?

This takes us to another question: what are 'creative' pursuits? Certainly, I do not merely mean hobbies. Being creative means indulging in something that we feel passionate about; it means making use of that special gift (as we have all been endowed with different but special gifts) – whether that is carving a face out of a piece of stone, planting a sapling in the ground and seeing it grow into a tree or developing a vaccine in a laboratory.

In order to be creative, we need to stop burdening ourselves with an otherwise busy existence. Remember that Archimedes (he – of 'eureka' fame) came up with the law of floatation whilst having a leisurely bath! And if it is a busy life we must lead, we should at least seek a measure of solitude, those rare times when it is just us. How many moments of reflection do we allow ourselves to enjoy, each year? Those quiet moments, away from the maddening crowds, can be so therapeutic because they allow us to rediscover ourselves and to reorientate our lives. Unless I am mistaken, I think that it was Buddha who said that "time doing nothing is never wasted"!

I reach the inevitable (and probably rather obvious) conclusions that:

a. being creative is far preferable to a prescribed professional existence; and

b. allowing ourselves some solitude and a few moments of reflection is not only valuable but absolutely necessary, particularly in a busy life.

And yet, most of us still lead a busy and breathless life. The leisurely pace from a few years ago has been replaced by a much more hurried life. I remember when I first started working in the mid-'80s, I would send a letter to a client and, probably two weeks later, I would receive a response. Now, if I do not receive a response to an email by the end of the day, I start to worry – has my email gone astray?

So, why has the pace of life (in every aspect) increased so dramatically? There is no question that we have advanced in many different ways because, as human beings, we always strive for something better. It was exactly this inquisitive nature that led Prometheus to steal fire from the Olympian gods in order to give it to the human race. Just like ourselves, Prometheus spurred himself on by looking at the gods and tormenting himself by the thought that they had possession of fire whereas he and the rest of humanity were deprived of it. Therefore, he had to have it! Prometheus's desire to better himself and consequent brave action (some might say act of folly) then led to his cruel punishment by Zeus. According to the myth, Prometheus was nailed on a rock face and a vulture was despatched to eat his immortal liver which constantly replenished itself so that the punishment would be repeated every day for eternity.

Notwithstanding our knowledge of Prometheus's fate, we still crave a richer life, full of knowledge and adventure. These are the things that fulfil us as human beings. However, I cannot help but wonder if, on the way, we have not lost our peace of mind. Our lives have become frenetic – running from one event to the next, wanting one more purchase after another and utilising dozens of different forms of communication. The recent onslaught of social media on our lives has exacerbated this non-stop way of living, tenfold. Running, running – always running!

Wanting to better ourselves is of course admirable and inevitable, but have we lost something precious along the way? Have we lost that moment of reflection – or what I would call our tranquility?

The chrysalis could not have stayed in its cocoon, but has it flown too far into the wind?

THE ECONOMIC CYCLE

Ever since the Liz Truss debacle (I would not go as far as to call it a government), there has been markedly reduced economic activity in the country. The International Monetary Fund (IMF) is reporting that the UK economy has contracted since last year, and in April 2023, it continues to retain its position as the worst-performing leading economy in the world. Rishi Sunak would prefer to blame either Covid or Russia's invasion of Ukraine for this. Others in the property industry might refer to a myriad of other issues such as the government's consultation on the calamitous update to the National Planning Policy Framework (NPPF) (which proposes the removal of the requirement for housing targets), the increase in the cost of construction materials, lack of a workforce brought about by Brexit and so on. The end result is that, little over ten years since the last recession (which was a result of the banking crisis, in that instance), we are again faced with reduced economic activity and a cost of living crisis. Amusingly, it is not called a recession this time; instead, people use the euphemistic term of 'strong economic headwinds', which makes it sound a little more palatable.

The latest crisis is confirmation, if any were needed, that the economy goes through regular cycles of boom and bust. Such a regular burden is a little like that of the mythical Sisyphus who was punished by the Olympian gods to repeatedly roll a rock up a hill, only for the rock to roll back down again as soon as Sisyphus had managed to reach the top. He would then start again…

The trouble about this cycle is that it significantly affects people's lives. It is not merely an event that happens and then passes. It is something monumental that leaves human wreckage in its passing. I knew people during the last recession in 2008/2009 who not only lost their jobs, but they also lost their families and livelihood; some lost their minds; and others lost their lives. These are the people whom we leave behind as the more fortunate amongst us manage to regain a little of our composure in order to start rolling the rock up the hill, one more time.

All this begs the question: are we correct in simply accepting this? What can we do about this cycle that economists tell us is inevitable? They also tell us that it is all dictated by *the market.* Who/what is the market? I would like to meet him/her/it one day! How come we have allowed it to determine our lives? And finally, is there a way out of the capitalist system that we live and operate in?

These are very big questions that a mere mortal like me cannot find answers to. However, the inability to comprehend these market forces does not stop me from toiling away in order to give myself, my family and those around me the chance to be able to control our lives, as far as we can. We may be nothing but pawns to the financial system, but even whilst down, I choose to retain my dignity and my positivity. In fact, I would go as far as to say that, rather than bemoan the occasional hardships of the economic cycle, we should redouble our efforts to confront them! It is these bad times which inevitably make us learn; they make us stronger and better able to face the next downturn.

We may be in the clutches of a beast (isn't this the same beast that had so preoccupied Franz Kafka, even before the capitalist system itself?) which, I for one, do not understand nor will I ever accept. Nevertheless, I refuse to dwell on either the beast or the hardship that it imposes on us. I'd rather focus instead on the brighter days ahead. Consequently, no matter how downtrodden we become during the gloomy cycle, I refuse to let it beat me. I maintain a smile on my face. Why?

It's all to do with the myth of Persephone! She was the much-loved daughter of Demeter, who was the goddess of agriculture. One day, as she was busy picking flowers in the fields, Persephone was abducted by Hades, the ruler of the underworld, who bundled her onto his chariot and then took her with him to the Land of the Dead. Demeter was devastated and pleaded with Zeus to persuade Hades to let Persephone come back to her. Zeus replied that he could not do that because, by that time, Hades had given Persephone a pomegranate to eat, and that signified abandonment. Demeter was furious and, being the goddess of agriculture, she brought havoc on earth; nothing would grow, and the people perished. This forced Zeus to suggest a compromise to the two parties: Persephone to stay for six months with Hades in the underworld, but she would then return to her mother on earth for the last six months. This was all agreed, but Demeter had the last word for, during Persephone's stay on earth, Demeter would allow nature to flourish; those are the seasons of spring and summer. On Persephone's return to Hades, gloom and greyness would engulf the world; those would be the seasons of autumn and winter.

Despite its undertones of doom, I love this myth because it signifies *regeneration*. Each time that the dark economic clouds appear on the horizon, I remind myself that Persephone is just on her way. She will bring about the greening of the trees, the bursting of beautiful flowers through the ground and the return of bright sunshine that will fall generously on our weary faces. Particularly during times of hardship, it is worth remembering that spring is but a few moments away.

CORNUCOPIA

My family have recently returned from a short holiday in the Loire Valley, France. We all fell in love with the beauty of the region. A majestic river surrounded by lush countryside with rows and rows of vineyards, golden fields of wheat or just natural woodland. Birds tweeted away, without any care in the world. Dotted around this magnificent landscape were picture-postcard villages.

This scene brought to my mind the myth of the Horn of Plenty (otherwise known as Cornucopia). When the Olympian god Zeus was a baby, his mother hid him away in a cave somewhere on the island of Crete. A goat, named Amalthea, used to provide him with his daily milk. One day, the playful baby broke a horn off Amalthea, and from that day on, all sorts of food and rich nourishment would pour out of it in order to provide the baby Zeus with his required nutrition. Ever since then, Cornucopia has symbolised prosperity, wealth and abundance and is associated with the harvest and thanksgiving. As a footnote, Zeus is said to have so loved Amalthea that he placed her among the stars as the constellation of Copia. Today we know her as Capricorn.

Returning to the Loire Valley – in addition to its natural beauty, the other thing that struck me about this region was its quiet! The quiet of nature (other than the chirping of birds and the gentle sound from the flowing river) was understandable. However, what I found both puzzling, and to a certain extent disturbing, was the quiet in each of the villages that we went to. There were hardly any people about! There may have been a smattering of shops but (other than the odd boulangerie), hardly any of those were open. In one village I saw a lady picking vine leaves that were overhanging her garden fence but nobody else. Where were the people?

These scenes reminded me of another trip I had made to Sicily a few years ago. I was with a group of friends and all of us remained open-mouthed at the sheer beauty of the island. Besides the natural beauty which could not have been bettered, each village was utterly beguiling in its construction and layout. Nothing appeared to be out of proportion. You just wanted to stand there and stare at the beauty of each village for ever! And yet, just like my more recent experience in the Loire, there was hardly anyone there. In one case there was one black-clad old lady sitting on the kerb outside her humble dwelling but literally no one else. It was almost eerie. Everyone else had emigrated to either Rome or New York.

I was left surprised and perplexed that people would abandon such cornucopias for the lure of a buzzing city, and I discussed this matter with my son.

"Why do you think there are no people in the Loire Valley?" I asked him one day, and the answer came back with immediacy:

"There is no Wi-Fi here!"

So that was it. The ability to connect (whether electronically or by transport) was clearly a big factor. My son then went on:

"Plus, there's nothing to do here. I could spend a few days looking at the vineyards and listening to the birds, but after a while I would be bored."

This got me thinking. If this is what people want, why do we not provide more of these facilities in the countryside? Why do we not provide more cafes, shops and some employment in places such as these that are 'heaven on earth' so that we end up with both natural beauty *and* facilities? Conversely, should we not try and recreate nature in the new human settlements that we build? I suspect this is what prompted Ebenezer Howard to start his garden cities movement some one hundred years ago. Letchworth and Welwyn eventually emerged. How successful have these been and, if not successful, what were the reasons of our failure to create 'cities in a garden'?

We have of course continued to experiment with garden cities in a noble attempt to create 'cornucopia'. As a result, we have had George Osborne's renewed efforts as chancellor which led to garden villages in Bicester and Ebbsfleet – amongst many others, not only in the UK but several good examples around the world as well. All this has been happening whilst the perennial question of brownfield vs greenfield has been occupying our profession as well as our politicians. Despite all these valiant efforts, it is clear that the garden city/village movement has not been transformative. Patches of excellence here and there, but the rest of the world carries on unperturbed. Probably the best illustration of this is the prediction that by 2050 some 70% of the world's population will be living in cities.

More recently, there has been a fresh initiative to bring nature to our urban environments. In particular the Dutch, as well as some other Northern European countries, have taken to introducing orchards into new settlements. These are tended by the new residents who benefit not only as a result of the production of fruit but also because such activities are relaxing and reduce the stress of an otherwise busy existence. The UK has also responded to this challenge through the introduction of legislation relating to Biodiversity Net Gain which was introduced in February 2024.

The big question is: are we succeeding in our efforts, or should we just accept that cities and countryside have two very different roles? If you want a busy life, you stay in the city, but if you want a more leisurely way of life, you need to stay in the countryside. You couldn't bring more and more facilities to the countryside because that would most likely destroy it. If that is the case, does it then come down to a question of choice?

This dilemma is aptly illustrated by one of Aesop's fables (yes, they were asking the same questions 2,500 years ago!). The fable goes like this:

A country mouse invited a town mouse to pay him a visit and enjoy the country life. As they ate their roots and wheat stalks, the town mouse said to his friend: "How can you eat such dull food? In my house, I am surrounded with every luxury; if you come with me, you can share my gourmet fare." The country mouse agreed and returned to town with his friend. On their arrival, the town mouse placed before the country mouse different pieces of delicious food, including bread, figs, honey and cheese. Much delighted at the sight of such good cheer, the country mouse expressed his satisfaction and bemoaned his own dreary life. But just as they were about to start eating, someone opened the kitchen door and they both ran off as fast as they could. They had scarcely returned to their feast when a cat appeared and the two mice, more frightened than before, ran away again. At last, the country mouse, now famished, said to his friend: "Although you have promised me a delicious feast, I am leaving you to enjoy it yourself. It is surrounded by too many dangers and distractions. I have lost my peace of mind here; I'd rather have my wheat stalks and roots and enjoy the peace that the countryside offers me."

So, it *does* appear that it comes down to a question of choice. However, were we to dig deeper, would this presumption stand up to scrutiny? Let's take as one simple example what has happened in the area between Vauxhall and Waterloo in South London over the last twenty years or so. I have witnessed with my own eyes the complete transformation of this area into a concrete jungle of high-rise buildings. Yes, it has been the reuse of decaying brownfield land, but what has been put in its place is grotesque and the complete antithesis of the natural environment which I had experienced in the Loire. What makes this calamitous urban environment even worse is its affordability (or rather lack of affordability). Such an offering means that it does not really come down to choice, because most people aren't able to afford it. At the same time, most people aren't able to buy a house in the countryside – therefore, economics is a significant constraint on our free choice. The irony about this is that there is a small proportion of people who are able to buy a *second* home in the countryside, which of course has its own consequences, including additional quiet during a large part of the week!

Since the late '80s, another factor has emerged which suggests to me that it is no longer a question of choice, and that is climate change. As temperatures rise, many cities are becoming too hot for comfortable living. Buildings and roads tend to absorb sunlight and trap heat. As a result, the temperature of urban areas is often several degrees higher than the surrounding countryside. Hence cities need to fight back if they are to survive. In fact, London is already following many other cities by setting up 'cool spaces'; it is also planting more trees.

Will this be enough? I have a feeling that 'tinkering at the edges' is no longer the answer and we will soon be left without any choice at all. Survival is the existential question. Therefore, the only choice left for us is to allow nature (whether in cities or in the countryside) back into our lives. It's not a question of one or the other; it's a question of recognising the importance of nature and building our settlements accordingly. Furthermore, we have entered a digitised world which suggests a possible integration of urban and rural living, dependent on both physical and virtual connectivity. This should satisfy my son!

I conclude that we should urgently agree new rules of engagement (for both countryside and city living).

This will require shared principles and measures, and it will mean behavioural change and new ways of building communities. Civil society, with not-for-profit and community-interest companies, should become the platform for this new undertaking – otherwise we may become irrelevant.

So, where does all this leave Amalthea? Will Amalthea's horn stop pouring out all the different products that make human life worthwhile?

Only Zeus knows the answer to this vital question, and now that he has reached maturity, he will surely make the right decision…

THE GIFT

The story of Pandora is known by most people. According to Hesiod, Pandora could not contain her curiosity and she hurriedly opened a gift that mischievous Zeus had given to her and her husband. This released sickness, death and many other evils into the world. For a long time, I have wondered how a mere gift (particularly a very special gift given to you by a god) can have such a devastating outcome. In this context I have thought about many people who, even though highly gifted, are at some point found to contain, just like Pandora's box, a scandalous secret or to have had a particular proclivity towards something which, in many cases, could be seen as a grave personal flaw.

The most obvious example of this is the composer Richard Wagner who is considered to be a musical genius, even though he was anti-Semitic at the same time. Philip Roth, the giant of modern American literature, was horrible to his different wives/female partners. Similarly Ted Hughes, whose behaviour was allegedly a contributing factor to Sylvia Plath's suicide. Then there is Alexander the Great who killed his best friend in a drunken stupor. Ryan Giggs, even though a sublime footballer, had an affair with his brother's wife whom he later married and is now accused of mistreating her. Even Churchill, the great leader and victor of the Second World War, had contempt for Mahatma Gandhi and regarded the Indian people to be inferior to the British. Gauguin may have slept with young women. The list is endless…

All this is certainly disappointing to many of us because we somehow expect our heroes to be exemplary human beings as well as brilliant in their chosen field. So, when the truth comes out of the box, we are flattened! However, the bigger question is: why do these gifted people do it? Why, despite their 'special gift', is there this other side to them?

The answer may be that all of us (even you and I, mere insignificant human beings who were born to toil away on a daily basis without any bestowment of a special gift) harbour different demons within us. Some of these demons are grotesque; others may be less so, but nevertheless they are there!

The next big question is: do these personal proclivities and/or flaws affect the work of gifted people, and should it diminish their standing in, and contribution to, the world? What does it matter that Leni Riefenstahl made Adolf Hitler into a hero in her film *Triumph of the Will*? Is she not still a great artist? Lord Mountbatten had a very complicated private life; does that prevent him from being the icon of British royalty? By all accounts Tolstoy was a very difficult husband; does that mean that his *War and Peace* is not a masterpiece? Alfred Hitchcock had a habit of bullying his (often very beautiful) female stars; does that diminish the greatness of his films?

All this assumes that we can easily divorce one's personal life from their work. Let's put one into one box and the other into another; the two are unaffected! But are they?

We can start by looking at Patricia Highsmith, the great American writer known for her misanthropy. Hasn't that misanthropy seeped into her books, most notably in her masterpiece *The Talented Mr Ripley*? Churchill's contempt of the Indians; did that not affect Britain's colonial policies, and did it not therefore shape the history of a nation? In modern times we have a minister (Matt Hancock) indulging in an extramarital affair and 'breaking the rules' when the whole country was attempting to exercise restraint because of Covid. How much of Hancock's behaviour has been a result of his own prime minister's lack of moral authority as illustrated by Boris Johnson's private life? And finally, nobody can deny that Salvador Dali's highly sexualised persona did not filter through to his work!

At the end of the day, a very few number of people (those whom we call great or geniuses) have been granted a gift – whether that gift is in literature, art, sport or leadership. They've got 'it', and we give them credit for that. In the same vein, should we not give them credit for their darker side? Is giving credit (for either their gift or for their personal flaws) important? Does it matter? It seems to me that Philip Roth's work can be enjoyed even if the name on the book cover was a different one. Similarly with Dali's signature on his paintings. So, we can attribute responsibility to all these flawed geniuses for their personal actions, but their work continues to matter because it is making a contribution to our world.

My conclusion – private proclivities and/or flaws do influence people's work (Dali, Pier Paolo Pasolini, etc.). The proclivities of such gifted individuals do not diminish their work; in fact, it may even be argued that, in some cases at least, without these personal frailties/demons, we would not have had great work (Gauguin, Fyodor Dostoevsky, etc.). That work does not of course excuse or justify their personal failings – particularly when those failings go on to affect the rest of the world (e.g. Churchill's view of India). In other cases, those failings remain a private matter (between Giggs and his wife) and the consequences are therefore less relevant to the rest of us. Having said that, we are still disappointed to see such people's inner demons externalised and can no longer watch the marvellous Ryan Giggs goal against Arsenal in the 1999 FA Cup semi-final without simultaneously thinking of him allegedly mistreating his wife.

So, the work of flawed geniuses is still important; it speaks to the rest of us and is therefore a contribution to the world. It gives us hope. That work does not belong to Salvador Dali, Philip Roth or Richard Wagner; it was merely a gift given to them which they then passed on to us.

What of Pandora and the catastrophic gift which had been bestowed to her? Thankfully, her story does not quite end with the unleashing of all ills to the world. Pandora was inconsolable for what she had done but, as she sat by the gift box crying, she heard a small sound from inside the box. She lifted the lid one more time and, at the bottom of the box, there was the most beautiful bird tweeting away. It was Zeus's ultimate gift to Pandora (and to the world). She opened the lid wide, and the little bird flew away joyfully into the skies. The name of that bird? Hope!

BETRAYAL

I first wrote this poem in Greek, in April 1980. I decided to translate it into English in 2022, as a result of two key events:

    a.   Brexit and the way we had allowed Boris to grow in our midst, believing that he was merely a lovable comedian – except that he fooled the country to vote for Brexit; and

    b.   Russian oligarchs whose money we took without much questioning. This led to our society being corrupted and to Ukraine being invaded.

I.
Erroneously
we let the few
dictate our lives!
We encouraged Ephialtes[2]
with our stadia, our theatres
and our agora.

---

2   *Ephialtes was a Greek who betrayed the three hundred Spartans at Thermopylae. He led the Persians who, for three days, had been unable to break through the pass at Thermopylae, round a secret path to the back of the Spartan defensive line.*

II.
So, almost inevitably,
one moonless night,
he took the rugged footpath
and brought the Persians.

III.
What does it matter now
that we have become
symbols of defiance?
What does it matter
when our city has fallen,
our temples have been desecrated,
our women enslaved?

IV.
We let Ephialtes
dine at our banquets,
pray at our festivals
and share our city with us,
believing that he was harmless.
Quietly,
he rose in our midst
and utterly destroyed us!

THE MINOTAUR

I have often wondered how and why certain myths continue to exert a hold on us, even thousands of years after they first emerged.

For me, one of the most fascinating of myths has been that of the Minotaur, the half-man half-bull creature that lived in the labyrinth. Over the years, I have on occasion stopped to consider a number of questions about this particular myth. How could a human mind conceive such a monster? What exactly gave rise to the beast and what is its significance? What is the myth trying to tell us?

The word Minotaur is derived from two Greek words – *Minos*, the king of Crete at the time, and *taurus*, which means bull. Hence Minotaur literally means the 'bull of King Minos'.

So, King Minos kept the Minotaur imprisoned in the labyrinth (a huge maze that nobody could escape from). One savage detail about the Minotaur is that he used to be fed with human captives who were regularly thrown into the labyrinth. The Minotaur was eventually killed by the young Athenian prince, Theseus, who had the help (inevitably) of King Minos's daughter Ariadne; it was she who had advised Theseus to enter the labyrinth by unrolling a ball of wool so that he would then be able to find his way out.

It is almost bewildering that the story of the Minotaur has gone on to inspire so many different artists. In particular, Picasso used it in many of his works (*Guernica* being one of them) as, to him, the Minotaur symbolised violence, guilt and despair – all of which alluded to the savagery that lies beneath the surface of civilised life. Jackson Pollock, William Blake and hundreds more similarly drew inspiration from this myth. Why this fascination with such a monstrous creature?

Notwithstanding this fascination, there is an even bigger question *behind* this myth, and that is the story of Daedalus and his son Icarus. Daedalus was the Thomas Heatherwick of ancient times and the architect of the labyrinth. In fact, King Minos was so pleased with the labyrinth that he decided to imprison Daedalus and Icarus so that they would not be able to reproduce anything approaching the brilliance of the labyrinth for anybody else! Daedalus of course could not stand imprisonment; he therefore used his skills and, by collecting the feathers from the different birds that used to nest on the roof of his

prison, he constructed wings for both himself and his son. They were therefore able to fly to freedom!

What I find particularly intriguing about this story is the relationship between the artist/designer and his client (King Minos). Is this relationship still relevant today, and is this why this myth remains so vibrant more than three thousand years later?

I will attempt to answer this question from my own experience, which I suspect is not dissimilar to many others'. As a consultant, I find that I always have to start from the 'brief'. Irrespective of my own views and beliefs, my work has to respond to the stipulations of a specific brief. You have to either work within those constraints or, alternatively, you simply walk away from it. There is no other option, and even though this is not quite to the same scale as Daedalus's imprisonment within the labyrinth, it is still restrictive.

It is not just consultants whose 'freedom' is constrained by the client's brief. I have worked with many public authority officers (the highway or planning officer) who, on many occasions, feel frustrated that they play second fiddle to their local politicians. These officers often know what the right thing to do is but, because of local politics, they have to lower their heads and keep quiet. Their voice is silenced with the result that their professionalism is, like Daedalus, chained.

To some, this might not appear such a hardship; it is simply the code that most professionals have to live by. There is, however, an even bigger loss of freedom in the case of many people who do not *enjoy* their jobs; they simply do it because they have to pay their bills. These people subject themselves to the drudgery of every day for no other reason than that they need the money. Their misery is of course worsened by the different layers of bureaucracy (similar to the endless corridors of the labyrinth) that they have to deal with. China has taken working practices to the extreme so that the working norm in China is now known as 996 – 9am to 9pm, six days a week. Personally, I could not conceive of such an existence, but there are millions of people who put up with (rather than enjoy) their job on a daily basis. Isn't this imprisonment, and how could one break free?

Would a possible course of action be for the Minotaur to pound the earth with his strong hooves and, with smoke coming out of his ugly nostrils, charge and break the confines of the labyrinth? What I am talking about is complete restructuring of our daily routines so that people's professional lives cease to be burdensome. Creativity and the joy of working need to be an essential part of everyone's professional life. However, wouldn't such a move actually break the capitalist system that we all function within? Is this really possible?

I am reminded of Franz Kafka's book, *The Trial*, in which the protagonist was battling a system that was both invisible and determined to crash him!

In fact, all this makes me think that the Minotaur may not be the victim; he may actually be the *perpetrator* of the crime! The Minotaur is the Big Machine that so many millions of people are enslaved by in their everyday, unfulfilling professional existence. He is the monster that feeds on the hapless humans who are thrown into, and are wandering helplessly around, the labyrinth. The savagery and violence of the Minotaur that so gripped Picasso is actually that of a way of life that constrains people's freedom – and then gobbles them up. It's that of a system which, in many respects, makes us prisoners and which, if we ever dared lift our heads and question its validity, punishes us ruthlessly.

So, is there any way at all to break free from the labyrinth? Perhaps Daedalus's method might fare better. Should we use our creativity and natural flair to find a way out of an unsatisfying professional life and fly joyously away to the skies? One would hope so, but how do people fly if they are constrained by social (and other) factors? That is another big question which may merit a separate article…

In the meantime, I will cling to Daedalus's wings – however fanciful that may be!

WALLS

Recently, I had the good fortune of visiting PEARL in East London. PEARL is the brainchild of Professor Nick Tyler of UCL and stands for Person Environment Activity Research Laboratory. It is a unique facility that explores the ways in which people interact with their environment (and by that I do not merely mean the built world as it would also include the cultural, social, sensory environments that might be represented in, or affected by, what is built). The laboratory creates different life-sized environments (a railway station, a high street, a town square) so that Prof Tyler and his team can examine how the brain responds to the information conveyed collectively to it by the various senses. In so doing, Prof Tyler's team can then figure out how to change the environment in order to stimulate a more favourable reaction.

This work is founded on the principle that there is a lot more to building our world than just engineering and/ or architectural standards. This is because of the way the human brain works (and we still have not managed to understand how the largest part of the brain functions)! The implication is that:

We are building our world without having fully appreciated the issues (which is probably why we look back every thirty to forty years and proclaim that we need to change our approach because the previous generation have got things wrong!); and

The basis of our work should really be *sensory* (rather than, for example, a mathematical equation).

The focus on sensory experience and/or human emotions is probably what made the ancient Greeks attempt to *personify* things like jealousy, beauty, melody and many other concepts which are fundamental to human nature. Hence we have the Furies (*Erinyes*) who represent vengeance; the nine Muses representing poetry, lyric song, literature and all the arts; Narcissus, a young man known for his beauty who, on seeing his own reflection in a lake, fell in love with it and stood staring at it for the rest of his life. After he died, in his place sprouted a beautiful flower bearing his name. Even Echo was a nymph who had been punished by the Olympian gods, never to speak her own words but only to repeat those of others. And many more…

Returning to today, the approach adopted at PEARL focusing on the investigation of human emotions and the brain's reaction to different senses seems to agree with what I recently read in a book, entitled *Movement* by Thalia Verkade and Marco Te Brömmelstroet. The book describes how the Dutch are attempting to 'take back their streets and transform their lives'. A line in that book chimes completely with Prof Tyler's undertaking: "Design to be based on the logic of sociologists and not necessarily that of traffic engineers".

The Dutch are of course not the only ones who are questioning the monolithic approach to transport planning and, more generally, the way that we tackle the design of the built environment. In the last few years, TfL has promoted the Healthy Streets Approach which attempts to put people and their health at the centre of how we design, manage and use public spaces. The approach uses ten different indicators and is founded on the premise that the experience of being on a street affects all human senses. Again, note the similarity with the Dutch approach and the striking move away from technicalities as our understanding of different senses (individually and in combination) increases and that then enables us to attach a more *sensory approach* to the design process. At this point I should say that TfL's approach is not, of course, unique. There have been similar experiments in many other parts of the world, including Australia and America.

Where does this leave the British Standards which are the bread and butter of every practitioner in the built environment profession? Where does it leave a traffic engineer's visibility splays, stopping sight distances, the outputs from their traffic models and the tracking of refuse vehicles?

Moving on to consider an even *wider* question: where does it leave all the different professions (engineers, planners, architects, economists, surveyors, etc.) and, more fundamentally, where does it leave the *interaction* between these professions? So far, most of us have been working in silos. The architect abides by his/her principles, the transport planners by theirs, etc. There is very little interaction and understanding of each other – merely a little frustration. This compartmentalisation of professions reminds me of a wonderful poem by a modern Greek poet, Constantine P. Cavafy, entitled 'Walls', which I quote below:

WALLS

Without consideration, without pity, without shame
They have built big and high walls around me.

And now I sit here despairing.
I think of nothing else; this fate gnaws at my mind.

For I had many things to do outside.
Ah why didn't I observe them when they were building the walls?

But I never heard the noise or the sound of the builders.
Imperceptibly they shut me out of this world.

C. P. Cavafy

Silos, walls, the narrowness of professions! Does this mean that our educational system, which for years has been trying to produce *experts*, has got things completely wrong? It would be far more sensible for our universities to be producing people with *knowledge* – rather than people with degrees (there is a chasm between the two words). And who is advising/dictating to the universities the kind of offer (its breadth and content) they should be advancing?

A system that leads to experts is productive in some ways but limiting in many more ways. Being an 'expert' in something automatically makes you think that you know everything and that you therefore resist other people's contributions. Would it not be more sensible to start from exactly the *opposite* standpoint: that we know very little? Or else, as Socrates famously said, "I know one thing, and that is that I know nothing". This would then constitute the platform for us to reach out to all other recesses of our brain, as well as to all other professions.

Would it not be better to try to produce more rounded professionals? Would it not be wiser to allow *every single part* of the brain to have a say, not only in our professions but also in the way that we conduct our lives?

Would that not be liberating?

IMPERIALISM

The island of Cyprus was a British colony until it gained its independence in 1960. I say *independence* when, in fact, the island, even seventy years later, continues to be British in many respects. For example, the vast majority of Cypriots speak English fluently. Language is by far not the only influence of Britain on the island. Most Cypriots follow the Premiership as fervently as any Mancunian will follow either of the two Manchester teams. Cypriot youngsters went crazy about the Spice Girls, and they all love Mr Fawlty (as well as Mr Bean). I distinctly remember when I first came to the UK in the mid-'70s, different relatives would give me lists of various items that they wanted me to purchase for them from Marks and Spencer and which I duly delivered to them at the end of each academic year when I returned to my family for the summer holidays. They no longer have to compose such lists because you can now find M&S stores in every major city on the island!

There is no doubt that, even if the island is not quite as British as a Cotswold village, it continues to be dependent on Britain. Is this unique to Cyprus? The answer is: of course not! There are many other countries around the world that continue (even after their so-called independence) to be reliant on their previous rulers (is this the right word)? The African French colonies look to France (with mixed feelings, no doubt) and so do the ex-colonies of Portugal, Holland, Germany, etc. One might say that even Britain is now reliant on, and certainly looks to, America for direction in many aspects of life – whether this is in military operations, culture or commerce. This phenomenon is otherwise and euphemistically called the 'special relationship'. The most recent manifestation of imperialism is of course China's incursion into Africa, as well as to many other parts of the world.

Several questions arise from all this, such as, does imperialism affect our own profession of the built environment and, in a wider context, is imperialism beneficial to humankind?

The first part of the question is easy to answer. Architecture and the built environment are undoubtedly affected by the imperial power. We can see this in the countless 'mock-English' neighbourhoods in many ex-colonies. We can see it in the use of English planning regulations and the application of British Standards in the Commonwealth countries. It is evident in the many Romanesque buildings that can be found around the world. The Spanish colonisation of the Americas has even given rise to *arquitectura neocolonial española* – a new movement which arose in the twentieth century....

The second part of the question is far more complex and more difficult to answer. Leaving slavery out of the present discussion as that is undoubtedly a separate and a far more repugnant issue, is imperialism a positive or a negative, i.e. is it beneficial only to the 'mother' country, or does the 'subject' also benefit from imperialism? In answering this question, I shall take two examples from ancient history. Alexander the Great had set out to conquer the then known world (he reached Persia and subsequently Afghanistan and the Indus River) in order, he claimed, to spread Greek culture to the rest of the world. In other words, he saw himself as benefactor, rather than conqueror! In reality, he learnt a great amount from the conquered peoples and, at one point, he even started to dress in Persian costumes. Unfailingly, he would also send to his tutor Aristotle back in Macedonia everything new that he would come across – whether that was animals, birds, spices or some scientific or mathematical idea and innovation (remember that Mesopotamia had developed a great civilisation long before many other regions in the world). As a result, Aristotle (and the rest of Greece) acquired much more knowledge.

The same happened when the Roman empire spread eastwards and conquered Greece. In that case, the Romans absolutely fell in love with Greek sculpture, theatre and philosophy, and they started to copy it. So much so that it is often said that Rome may have conquered Greece, but Greek culture conquered Rome! We see this reciprocal conquest in all the magnificent Roman temples and amphitheatres as well as in Roman literature. The most vivid example of that is Virgil's 'The Aeneid' which is based on Homer (a twentieth-century example of the same phenomenon is James Joyce's *Ulysses* which transplants Homer to Dublin) – in this way perhaps illustrating that 'reverse imperialism' can last for centuries.

So, is imperialism a two-way process, and should it therefore be welcomed? Does it work like osmosis? Is it an exchange of ideas/cultures/ways of life, or is it subjugation? Here in Britain, America has given us (amongst many other things) McDonalds, a military alliance in NATO and country music. Has all this been good for us? Could we have done better without them?

In the specialist field of the built environment that I work in, I have seen that we have borrowed many concepts from our imperialist friends. We gave up our traditional offices in order to move into business parks, and we abandoned our high streets in order to shop in hypermarkets and/or shopping centres. We similarly abandoned our theatres and little cinemas which lay undistinguished and largely unappreciated in different towns in order that we might enjoy the grander 'cinema experience' that Hollywood promised us in a multiplex cinema.

The above examples intentionally ignore some of the better things that we have taken from imperial America, such as some outstanding films, plays, literature, music, etc. It also ignores the fact that Britain has given back to America an inordinate amount in terms of artistic contributions, political support, scientific collaboration and so forth. I suspect that China can make the same claim when it comes to its foray into Africa. It could say that, without its financial support, African infrastructure would not be improved, and Africa's ore and other minerals could not be exploited for the benefit of not only China but also Africa itself. It could similarly claim that its modern reinvention of the Silk Road is nothing to do with Chinese interests and all to do with the benefit of the whole world.

Therefore, it would appear (at least on the surface) that imperialism is a two-way process – even though the benefits are enjoyed by one side or the other, depending on where the pendulum actually lies. The pendulum can be placed very much to one side's advantage, or it can be allowed to be more fairly located.

At this point I should say that I started writing this essay in the middle of 2021 but I then gave up on it as I felt uneasy about the direction it was taking. Somehow, I could sense that I was not getting to the heart of the matter. And then, at the beginning of 2022, Russia invaded Ukraine! That jolted me into the utter reality of imperialism, and I therefore decided to revisit my essay.

Russia's actions made me realise that imperialism is not the benign force that I had assumed. There is a much darker side to it. To start with, there is absolute destruction and death, and then there is occupation (should this be better called enslavement?). *Imperialism is not an osmosis between two parties; it's subjugation!*

So, looking back in history, the Persians and the Indians never wanted to be imbued in Greek culture by the forces of Alexander the Great; they had their own cultures. All the different peoples that had been conquered by imperial Rome were most certainly not happy that they were (literally and figuratively) thrown to the lions. The Africans, Indians and the people of the Caribbean would have been quite happy without being enslaved by the British empire. And finally, the people of Vietnam and Latin America (as well as more recently those of Afghanistan and Iraq) would probably have thrived by themselves without America reaching out to 'help them'.

This raises another big question: is imperialism founded on financial power? Does the imperial nation need to have a financial and/or military backbone?

Modern examples illustrate that imperialism is primarily founded on economic power. Let us look at Japan, whose constitution after the Second World War does not allow it to have offensive military forces. The same is true to some extent with Germany who, initially after the Second World War, was not allowed to have an army and, even now, its military capabilities are restricted. Despite this, both countries have 'conquered' many parts of the world, through their *economic* prowess. Conversely, Russia is not economically strong (from the point of view of the average Russian citizen) and yet, because of its nuclear capabilities, it seeks to be an imperial power. The conclusion is that either economic or military might (or both) are the foundations of imperialism. This is confirmed by the two examples from ancient history that I cited earlier.

However, the same two examples also illustrate one other very important facet of imperialism. The Greeks of Alexander the Great did not necessarily conquer Asia. It was Asian spices and mathematics that conquered Greece. Similarly, the Romans may have captured Greece through their military might, but it was Greek thought that prevailed and completely consumed and overpowered the Romans. Is this not also what happened with the new imperial power, America? It may look as though America has the upper hand, but it was The Beatles that conquered America. Similarly, it may appear that Latin America is economically dependent on America, but it is 'Latino' culture (its food, music, as well as way of life) that is gradually and steadily conquering the imperial power!

This takes us to the final question which is: can imperialism be defeated? It seems to me that imperialism can only be defeated by creativity and thought. The Cypriots will stop wanting to buy M&S underwear if they develop a smarter M&S themselves. Britain will become less and less reliant on America if it continues to produce a Shakespeare, a Newton or another The Beatles. And Africa will be able to fight off the Chinese incursion once it educates itself and gives opportunities to its people to create civilisations based on their undoubted talents, unique history and traditions.

I conclude that the world can evolve without one power introducing its own norms and imposing them on others. Once you dictate to people how they should live, what they should read and eat, you are immediately narrowing their domain; you are taking away their freedom. At the very least, that's stifling human creativity.

We can all learn from each other but not through subjugation.

HUBRIS

I've always been fascinated by this word that so captivated the ancient Greeks who loved to see their kings fall. A prime example is Oedipus, who reached the pinnacle by becoming the king of Thebes and yet, despite numerous warnings and wise counselling, he kept probing. Who am I? Where do I come from? Countless times he was told to drop his enquiries – "you will not like what you find", but he kept getting closer and closer to the fire. He was the king and, after all, he was the one who had outwitted and subsequently killed the mighty Sphinx. He was spurred on by his almighty power as well as by a sense of danger that so attracted him. Until, of course, the bitter truth was revealed to him: the king he had killed in a chance encounter several years before was his father and, by subsequently marrying the widowed queen, he in fact had married his own mother! There can be no better demonstration of hubris than this. The mighty king who feared no one ends up realising that he is the lowest human being imaginable – so much so that he digs out his own eyes. He cannot bear to look at the world anymore.

So, what does hubris *really* mean? Is it a characteristic of ancient times, or is it prevalent throughout all human history? What causes it? What are its consequences, and why does it seem to be carrying so much weight? Can it be resisted?

According to the dictionary, hubris means excessive pride verging on defiance of the gods and inescapably leading to nemesis. Perhaps some modern examples might explain the word a little better. The hapless Liz Truss illustrates hubris (and its consequences) perfectly. She was attracted to power and reached for the top crown, not because she had the ability but because she had been dazzled by the prize – only to fall unceremoniously very soon after her apotheosis (*theo* is a Greek word which means God; hence theology).

The world has of course been full of hubristic behaviour in ancient times and modern, and we can find it in every walk of life. Lance Armstrong, who had won seven Tour de France titles, wanted to keep winning, even after he knew that the doping investigators were on his tail. In his arrogance, he was almost tempting them to come after him and, inevitably, that brought about his downfall. Rudolph Giuliani was at one point the hero of the free world when, as mayor of New York, he responded with empathy and defiance to the 9/11 tragedy. His fall came twenty years later when he became Donald Trump's poodle, alleging fraud in the American presidential election. They had both reached a stage in their lives when they had started to believe that they were not accountable to anybody. Then there is Prince Andrew and his infamous interview with Emily Maitlis. He strode into the interview room as if he was untouchable; he was the prince, and he was going to show the rest of us how mistaken we were about him. His subsequent fall has been profound and excruciating. And so on…

Moving now onto our world of the built environment (developers, architects, engineers, planners, etc.) – is *that* world affected by hubris? Speaking from my personal experience, I can say that we are not immune to it. In my professional life, I have seen some people who, even though in their early careers may have been a little timid, subsequently develop into positions with power and, suddenly, they become much more confident and even brusque. They know that they are sitting at the top of the world, and so they become bullies. Nothing can touch them, and everything is possible for them. That's hubris.

It's not just individuals who may behave in this way; I have witnessed whole institutions and corporations that behave with arrogance and aloofness. This was particularly true of two major retailers that I worked for in the late '80s and '90s. In their case, if there was an obstacle to their business expansion plans, they behaved as though they could smash it to smithereens. There was a planning system, but they could defeat it with their army of top-quality consultants (legal advisors, planners and engineers). And what happened to those retailers eventually? They have been humbled. Other retailers have come onto the scene who have drained them of their power.

I am almost tempted to say that our behaviour towards tall buildings is, in many cases, similarly hubristic. There is no doubt that going high avoids urban sprawl and leads to more sustainable settlements. However, there are occasions when we build high simply because we want to show the rest of the world that we are able to reach the sky. We want to outdo the tall buildings that came before us. In those cases, are we not simply building towers in the sand? Likewise, is it not hubris that drives many dictators around the world to build huge and completely unnecessary palaces for themselves, when their countrymen are living in poverty? President Nicolae Ceausescu of Romania, Erdogan in Turkey, Putin in Russia…

All of this reminds me of the Tower of Babel. According to Genesis, the Babylonians wanted to make a name for themselves by building a mighty tower *with its top in the heavens.*

Building tall and building big for no reason other than that we wish to exercise (and demonstrate) power is the epitome of hubris. We of course know how the Tower of Babel ended up: in complete and utter collapse!

And so, we come to the big question: what causes hubris? Is it the communities and the political system that we live in? This cannot be so because we encounter it with kings (Oedipus), autocrats (Ceausescu) and democrats (Liz Truss). Are people born to be hubristic? There is no evidence of that; on the contrary and, looking at the example from the development industry that I quoted above, people become hubristic with increasing power. Some can control power, but others cannot; it engulfs them like a flame.

Finally, is there a 'cure' for hubris? Can there be redemption? This takes us onto *catharsis* – another Greek word which means 'cleansing'. Catharsis wipes out the ills of hubris and enables a fresh start. We have already seen this in the case of Oedipus, who had gouged out his own eyes and was subsequently taken round by his two daughters to show the rest of the world what hubris can do to man/woman. We have many more such examples but let's suffice ourselves with a modern one: Jonathan Aitken, who reached the higher echelons of political life in the 1990s and was at one point being talked of as the next leader of the Conservative party. Almost inevitably, he came tumbling down, following his legal case against *The Guardian*. His redemption came once he had found God, whilst in prison.

Is there an alternative to catharsis that might cleanse someone from hubris? Empedocles, a pre-Socratic philosopher who lived on the island of Sicily in the fifth century BC, thought that he had found a way. Empedocles took hubris to the highest level because he came to believe that he was a god – so much so that he flung himself into the volcanic crater atop Mount Etna in order to demonstrate his divinity to the crowd that had gathered around the rim of the volcano to witness his plunge.

The ancient Greeks used to say *pan metron ariston*, which in English translates loosely as 'everything in moderation'. Once you fail to control power, wealth and fame, the inevitable outcome is that hubris takes over your life and destroys it, utterly.

THE VANQUISHED

(based on Homer's 'The Iliad')

As the last of the Greek ships
disappeared into the dark night
and the vastness of the sea,
we looked wearily at each other.

We did not speak
for we knew what would follow.
We then
pulled ourselves up,
with our rags
hanging loosely from our ravaged bodies,
and we started to gather
everything that we had left.

It was not a lot.
One or two broken urns,
a couple of stanchions from our burnt homes
and the murdered dogs.
Priam's throne
had been smashed to smithereens.

Silent still,
we picked up, one by one, all its
broken pieces
and gathered them
in a humble heap,
in the middle of the Grand Room.
The next morning,
we saw standing in the middle
of the room
a dazzling throne,
imposing and authoritative.

This did not surprise us.
Nor did we think that
it was strange.
We were certain that
it would happen,
as we were certain that,
together with the bright sun
rising gloriously
from the Trojan horizon,
we too would rise.

Beaten and exhausted,
we would set off
to sow the fields
that stretched for miles
outside the city walls.

And so, with an absolute
certainty,
and without any fuss,
we would resume our lives,
as if nothing at
all had happened
in the previous ten years.

WHAT ARE WE GOING TO DO WITH HIGHWAY ENGINEERS?

People from outside my profession will invariably refer to my fellow professionals as highway engineers or transport planners and sometimes as just traffic consultants. There is a huge difference between these terms but, for the purpose of this article, I shall use the term 'highway engineer' to represent myself and all of my misunderstood fellow professionals.

Is the profession of highway engineering dead?

Why do I ask this question? First, a principal maxim in our profession is that "the more roads we build, the more traffic is created". It's a little like the mythological monster the Hydra – you chop one of its heads off and two more spring forth in its place! The same with roads – the more you build, the more traffic is created and therefore you need to build even more roads.

Hence highway engineers are confused – should they build more roads and keep providing traffic capacity, or should they seek to hinder it? More fundamentally, should highway engineers abandon their practice altogether?

Secondly, we are also being told that some aspects of current highway design are not appropriate. For example, wide carriageways and/or large bell mouths that prioritise the movement of buses or refuse vehicles create disadvantageous conditions for pedestrians; designing highway features in this way should therefore be abandoned. More fundamentally, should highway engineers simply stop designing?

And thirdly, as we all know, future technologies as well as changes in lifestyle (as a result of either Covid or the climate change crisis) will supposedly make cars redundant; so, there will no longer be the need to cater for the car! Is this the end of the road for highway engineers?

Let us consider this question from first principles. A highway engineer's work begins with traffic modelling. However, if capacity is no longer a priority, will we no longer have to carry out traffic modelling to try and establish future traffic conditions which will then help us design the correct highway network? If we were to do that, would it not result in traffic chaos? Suppose that it did; would that matter? Another maxim that is often quoted is that traffic 'will balance itself out', and it will find its own solution (probably by travelling at different times). So, let it be!

Then we come to certain fundamentals of highway design itself. Take visibility splays, for example. Many people are telling us standard visibility splays sterilise valuable land and a more compact junction design is preferred. Will we no longer care about providing adequate visibility splays at junctions? Would this not lead to many accidents and deaths? This fear presupposes that inadequate visibilities would cause accidents, and yet we know that there are many situations with significantly reduced visibility which actually lead to no accidents because people drive more carefully.

So, we can do without any traffic modelling and without certain fundamentals of highway design that ensure both safety and traffic capacity. Does all this mean the death of highway engineering? It most certainly does not, as we will still need highway engineers to design our bridges and our motorways. However, in cities and all new settlements, can we abandon the traditional way of designing roads? Would it mean the death of highway engineering in *those* situations?

It certainly means that highway engineers need to change. It means that we need to ask ourselves different questions. For example:

Instead of asking ourselves the question, "will this be safe?", we should be asking, "in addition to safety, will our design advance health and well-being?".

Instead of asking, "will this maximise traffic capacity?", we should be asking, "have we done as much as possible to promote walking, cycling and public transport – even if this is at the expense of traffic capacity?".

Instead of paying scant attention (and lip service) to the natural environment, we should seek to work with nature, capitalising on natural assets and delivering environmental net gain.

Instead of doing things "just like we have always done", we should seek to embrace and, if possible, anticipate, technological advances.

All this, of course, means that the role of the highway engineer will need to become something very different. Is this a threat or an opportunity?

In my view, it is certainly a threat which should, and can, be turned into a huge opportunity. Why? It is now abundantly clear that we live in an interconnected world. The old boundaries are crumbling, and in our sphere of building and construction, there are a great number of issues that affect each other. For example, one of the most significant pollutants is carbon emissions from traffic. Highway engineering is therefore directly linked to the climate change crisis.

Similarly, obesity and a multitude of other health problems are the result of people driving, instead of walking or cycling (and it is heartening that the ex-PM Boris Johnson believed that bikes should be prescribed on the NHS and that "our bike lanes could become huge, twenty-four-hour gyms which are free and open to everyone"). Again, this is directly linked to highway engineering and perhaps suggests a different emphasis (creating green corridors instead of stark carriageways for cars) to the way that highway engineers might approach their work.

Finally, technology is changing the way we move. Whether we are talking about electric cars or autonomous vehicles or e-scooters, it still comes back to how engineers design the highway. In other words, do highway engineers need to become multi-modal engineers by default?

All this is telling me that, far from being dead, highway engineering is beginning to take *centre stage*! It will no longer be enough for highway engineers to know their British Standards and to then apply them in designing roads. In future, highway engineers will need to be scientists (to understand new technologies); doctors (to appreciate the effect of their designs on human health); environmentalists (to be mindful of any contribution they might make to climate change) and much more. In other words, highway engineers will need to emerge from their silo and approach future challenges in a much more holistic way.

However much we may wish for it to happen, the car will not go away. A recent report by the Institute for Public Policy Research has concluded that there will be 25% more cars on the roads by 2050 as the shift to electric vehicles causes a congestion crisis. Therefore, highway engineers will still need to design for car movement, but the emphasis of their work will have to change from that which makes everything possible for increased traffic capacities to one that attempts to 'tame' the car.

Much more than that, however, highway engineers will need to spread their wings and, even more importantly, they will have to raise their voices. We will have to challenge ourselves (and all other fellow professionals around us) to start thinking in new ways. We will simply need to show leadership and to make sure that we are at the forefront of asking the big questions and providing solutions to the big challenges that we (and the whole world) will be facing.

How we will do that is another big question, but here are three starters for ten:

Create greater consistency in engineering syllabi at universities so that our future engineers are more aware and knowledgeable about wider issues, such as people's health and well-being; the environmental agenda, etc. Carbon literacy must be a compulsory subject!

Introduce different metrics into a highway engineer's work. Instead of relying entirely on numbers to do with traffic capacities, we should also have numerical grading of (for example) the extent of landscaping and green linkages and a standardised means of assessing cycle infrastructure.

Change an engineer's mindset so that they can break free from the narrow confines of their remit. Instead of satisfying ourselves with the debilitating, "I am just the highway engineer", we should start thinking of ourselves as the creators of the world that we live in.

In conclusion, I believe that highway engineering is about to undergo a transformational change. If the profession rises to all these different challenges, it could become the lynchpin of so many other professions and the catalyst for building better places (instead of just designing and building roads for cars). In fact, highway engineering could instead become 'Infrastructure Master-planning' or simply: '**Place-making**'.

THE AGORA

We all know what makes a good place – or rather, we all recognise a good place when we see one. It's those sun-drenched Italian squares, full of bustle, small pools of people conversing loudly and groups of children (let's call them street urchins) playing football amongst it all. It's also those Northern European neighbourhoods, neat and orderly with lots of beautiful landscaping (and the odd orchard thrown in the mix) and cyclists dominating the streetscape. It's the chaotic scenes that confront a Western visitor at an Asian market, loud, colourful and a little shambolic for our own Western taste.

We all rejoice in such places, and many of us want to copy them. We write whole essays about them trying to teach each other about what appears to be an elusive art of 'place-making'. The concept originated in the 1960s when writers such as Jane Jacobs offered groundbreaking ideas about designing cities that catered to people, not just cars and shopping centres. Other people soon followed, including Jan Gehl, who proclaimed, "First life, then spaces, then buildings – the other way round never works" – not forgetting Aristotle of course who, several thousand years ago, stated that "a city should be built to give its inhabitants security and happiness".

And so, we now have a multitude of noble approaches – Anne Hidalgo's (or should it be Professor Carlos Moreno's) 15-minute city, Barcelona's Superblocks, Melbourne's 20-minute neighbourhoods and (many years ago now) the Dutch woonerf, a social-architectural concept which considered new ways of living. Even Tirana's kid-friendly urban policy represents the spearhead of a grand plan to refashion Albania's capital city as a more sustainable and better place. All these different methods are striving for the same thing – and they have all resulted in approaches which move away from standard engineering formulae and closer to what one might call the 'human' angle. As a consequence, we have the Liveability Index in Melbourne, the Healthy Streets Approach which had been developed at TfL, the Walk Score in America and so on.

The big question is: why do we still fail to build better places? Why, despite so many people's noble efforts, do we continue to create lifeless residential neighbourhoods and unattractive squares? Why is a good place still the exception to the rule – the odd one out that merits a special visit by professionals, rather than the everyday standard which is enjoyed by everyone?

Or put in another way, how can we achieve better places, better communities and better living? What ingredients are essential to successful place-making? In my discussions with many people and in reading different books in an effort to answer this question, I have come across words which are familiar to, and often quoted by, people who are more knowledgeable in this subject than myself: words such as Vision, Long-term Strategy, Quality, Public Engagement, Stewardship, the Environment and so on. These are all very important. Below, I identify five that are my *personal* favourites.

Leadership must be at the very top of any list. Leadership provides direction and inspiration. It requires courage and someone who is prepared to lift their head above the parapet in order to do what is right. A leader must not waiver; their conviction will bring all others along. There are several such examples, but it will suffice for me to mention the regeneration of London Docklands under the command of the 'Tarzan of English politics' Michael Heseltine.

Time to successfully implement a particular project is of paramount importance because nothing can be achieved overnight. It therefore requires patience and a long-term strategy with different pieces falling into place on the way. Often, a long-term strategy is sacrificed for the sake of short-term opportunistic policies but, reassuringly, we still have many examples where different cities have avoided the temptation of short-termism in order to deliver something exceptional. Wulf Daseking was the city planning officer (*oberbaudirektor*) in Freiburg for nearly three decades, and the outcome is admired throughout the world; remember that Sir Peter Hall had labelled Freiburg as the "new Jerusalem".

An integrated approach is also required. What does this mean? It means architects, planners, engineers, economists working *together* rather than separately. A significant obstacle to that is the existing *compartmentalisation* of professions. It is high time that all the built environment disciplines came out of their silos and worked collegiately as a team of *builders*. This will spark various (and surprising) ideas and will undoubtedly deliver a project which will have been considered from any number of different perspectives. It is probably as a result of this more integrated approach that several Northern European countries are now giving greater prominence to *nature* in the places that they build. Their landscape architects (and their sociologists) are having a greater say in the design process.

Partnerships between a number of key stakeholders will provide focus and momentum to any project. Partnerships should be created at different levels from grassroots (engaging meaningfully with the people who will be using and living in that space) all the way up the hierarchy to different government departments, institutions, funders and developers. A notable example of this is Eindhoven's 'triple helix' partnership which consists of the mayor's office, the local university and private sector.

Cars is the big elephant in the room. The nominal report Traffic in Towns long ago warned that we needed to "tame this beast that we all love" for otherwise it would come to dominate our lives – and it has done. Everything that we build is predicated on the requirements of the car. Thankfully, this dependency is now being increasingly questioned and, having had a period of introducing carrots (more cycle lanes and better bus provision), councils in England are now wielding the stick – whether this is in the form of congestion charging, Clean Air Zones (as in Birmingham, Bath, Bristol and many more), Ultra Low Emission Zones (ULEZ) as in London or, more recently, Low Traffic Neighbourhoods (LTNs). There are countless more schemes around the world attempting to curb the influence of the car. Notable amongst these is Pontevedra in Galicia where the mayor boldly banned cars from most of the city in 1999. The city has since been reaping the rewards in reduced car accidents, reduced air pollution, plus an influx of some fifteen thousand residents into the city.

So, have I succeeded in outlining a recipe for successful place-making? Somehow, I do not think so! My recipe breaks down when one considers London's Borough Market and thousands of other similar places. Borough Market is in most respects a very successful place as it is often thronging with (happy and loud) people; it is vibrant and very popular. And yet it did not come about through any particular leadership or as a result of a long-term strategy, nor is it in any way a green project or one that is endowed with good-quality materials. It is just a place under a few railway arches, next to a busy highway. Nobody really planned it in any sense that we know; it just grew *organically*, almost of its own accord.

Does London's Borough Market mean that we (the designers of places) have no role to play? If good places simply happen, why don't we just give up? The answer is that, notwithstanding Borough Market (and several other similar places), there are countless more places that prove the opposite. An obvious such example is the regeneration of King's Cross/St Pancras which, by the late twentieth century, had become a symbol of blight and decay, with derelict buildings, railway sidings and contaminated land. How was the subsequent successful regeneration achieved? In addition to the vision for the site (encapsulated in the document 'principles for a human city'), success came as a result of a strong partnership between the developer

Argent St George and the landowners, who were London and Continental Railways and Exel. This point also identifies the huge significance of *land ownership and its assembly:* every masterplan starts with many good intentions but, inevitably, all of them will be confronted with the Herculean task of multiple land ownerships. This leads not only to delays but, crucially, to the complete dismantling of the idea of a unified project; hence the breaking-up of what space is available.

The conclusion is that we can *facilitate* the creation of good place-making – just like we can (if we allowed greed to predominate) create monstrous jungles, as evidenced by what has been created in Vauxhall over the last twenty years.

Notwithstanding our own meagre contribution, it is clear that what really makes a successful place is the *people.* It is the people who make a place (in the same way that a place shapes people). For a place to flourish, it needs people who care about their community, who have moral values (what are these?), who believe in themselves, who have aspirations, who…

All these attributes are beyond the control of a place-maker but, nevertheless, they constitute the most essential element to what we are, almost in vain, trying to build. This reminds me of Epicurus, the philosopher who is wrongly remembered for advocating pleasure when in fact he had been asking a more fundamental question: how could people achieve happiness? He concluded that one essential ingredient is *friendships,* i.e. the community that we create and function within.

Does this mean that we (the built environment professionals) are redundant? Are we really never going to achieve the elusive chimera of a 'good place'? The answer of course is *no* – we will deliver good places, so long as we do it with people in mind. This means we should design places *with* the people and *for* the people. There can be no better representation of that (certainly in my own eyes) than the agora in ancient Athens where the space and the people gave rise to something that continues to enrich our lives to this day. When we say people, we mean *active citizens*, as encapsulated in the famous quote by Pericles: "We do not say that a man who shows no interest in politics is a man who minds his own business. We say that he has no business in our polis,[3] at all."

This quote makes it clear that good place-making is not quite enough; it also requires appropriate contributions from the people who use that place. It's the blend of the two that goes on to create human civilisation.

---

3   *Polis in Greek means 'city' – and the use of the word*
     'politics' by Pericles does not mean politics as we know it
     today. It means a citizen who is active in the affairs of his/
     her polis.

ATLANTIS

The myth of Atlantis is probably known by most people, and the story has been so captivating that some people have even gone in search of Atlantis. However, very few people will have paid due attention to the word 'myth' which is very significant, because that is exactly what Atlantis is – a *myth*!

It comes as a surprise to most people to know that Atlantis only existed in the imagination of Plato. One would have expected Plato to be tackling philosophical questions such as 'what is justice?' and 'how can one lead a moral life?' – and yet, with Atlantis, he appears to be indulging in what must have seemed at the time to be science fiction.

However, there are very good reasons for Plato's indulgence, as I will be explaining in this article. His Atlantis story is not merely science fiction, and it is as relevant to our world today as it was to Athens in the fifth century BC, when Plato wrote this myth. The story appears in one of his many dialogues (which are actually a lot of fun and not the heavy reading that one might fear and expect) called *Critias*, and it goes like this:

A very, very long time ago, there used to be a land which was the closest to heaven on earth. The wealth of the kings of Atlantis was staggering; their mineral resources were excellent; there was a plentiful supply of timber; every kind of domesticated and wild animal including elephants lived on this land; and the earth produced food in abundance.

Atlantis had temples, gardens, gymnasia, a hippodrome, a palace and a harbour. There was also an artificial ditch that channelled the river waters from the mountains to the city and onto a network of canals that provided transport infrastructure as well as irrigation. There were barracks for the soldiers and housing settlements for all the people who lived on Atlantis. It is interesting that Plato does not make mention of high-rise towers with exclusive apartments targeted at overseas sheikhs and oligarchs, but let us stay with the story!

One of the most fascinating aspects of this story is Plato's attempt to define what he considers to be an 'ideal place' – something which he repeatedly does in much of his writing. In addition to laws and governance, he goes into a lot of detail describing the *physical* characteristics of such a place which (he says) should have temples, orchards, a water system, a grid structure (was he thinking of Milton Keynes?), a certain number of residential units and so on… Does this attempt by Plato to define a place in its physical manifestation sound familiar to the urbanists and city-makers of today?

In fact, in another of his dialogues, Plato even *calculates* how many people should inhabit the ideal place. In his view, there is one perfect number; if below or above that number, the city harmony would be disrupted in some way. I wonder what he would have made of our modern metropolises! In any case, there is no doubt that Plato's search for the perfect size for a human settlement is a result of his mathematical predilections and devotion to Pythagorean principles. The Pythagoreans (named after the mathematical genius, Pythagoras) believed that everything in our universe is dictated by numbers – something which of course has subsequently been illustrated by Newton and Einstein, amongst others, even if a lot of school children today would not agree!

Returning to Atlantis, Plato informs us that the kings of Atlantis were just, wise and moral – until the inevitable moral degeneration set in and the people of Atlantis then ceased to "be able to carry their prosperity with moderation". As a result, once the almighty god Zeus had perceived this degeneration and watched with dismay the conspicuous consumption of the people of Atlantis, he decided to punish them. This brings us onto the big catastrophe (was it a tsunami, an earthquake or a war against a foreign country? We do not know) which obliterated Atlantis. There have been hundreds of theories since then as to where Atlantis may still lie – such as maybe at the bottom of the Atlantic ocean, somewhere in the Mediterranean or even in a Scandinavian fjord.

However, the important question is not where the Atlantis lies but *why* did Plato write such a myth? The answer is simple: he was trying to warn his fellow citizens in Athens (who by that time had achieved a great civilisation) not to rest on their laurels. He was effectively saying to them that, just like the mighty Atlantis had been obliterated as a result of its citizens' moral degradation, the very same thing could happen to Athens.

Does this myth have any relevance to us today? You might say it is a little far-fetched, but I think that our world is experiencing its 'Atlantis moment'. Leaders with no moral compass, utter devotion to material gains and our own disregard of the natural environment…

It is this last point that is of particular concern. Despite repeated pleas from modern prophets (starting with Al Gore in the early '90s, and more recently with people such as David Attenborough and even the young Greta Thunberg), we pay no heed to their warnings. As a consequence, we continue to fill our oceans with plastic; we remain glued to our cars; we hunt and kill whales in order to satisfy a peculiar culinary proclivity; we burn coal; we destroy virgin forests…

We also remain stubbornly oblivious to stark warnings from our planet itself – such as huge forest fires, the irreversible melting of the ice caps and unusual floods. Are we going to continue to ignore all these warnings, in the same way that the ancient Athenians ignored Plato? Is there a tsunami just round the corner awaiting to engulf our own Atlantis?

COMMODITIES

I have just finished a book called *The Last Colony*. It was written by Philippe Sands who is a human rights lawyer and professor of law at UCL. The book is shocking. It tells the story of how Mauritius (which, in addition to the main island that we are familiar with, consists of several islets in the Indian Ocean) gained its independence from Britain in the mid-'60s. Except that it gained only *partial* independence. A cluster of islets in the Chagos Archipelago (such as Peros Banhos and Diego Garcia) continued to 'belong' to Britain, and they are still referred to (by Britain) as the British Indian Ocean Territory.

Why did Britain wish to retain control of those islets (and at the same time keep it a secret)? Britain did so under pressure from the United States, who wanted to turn one of those islets into a military base. This they have done, and the islet of Diego Garcia has been an American military base ever since.

Astounding as this story may be, there are two additional details that stand out. First, it was from this islet that American war planes would take off on their bombing missions to Iraq during the disastrous war against Saddam Hussein, in 2003. Secondly, and most alarmingly, all the indigenous people who had long lived on those islets were forcibly removed in the latter part of the 1960s.

Madame Liseby Elyse was one of the people deported, and she describes her experience as follows: "The administration told us we had to board the ship, leaving all our personal belongings behind except for one suitcase each. We were like animals and slaves in that ship. People were dying of sadness in that ship." Madame Elyse goes on to say that she was four months pregnant at the time, and by the time the ship had reached Mauritius four days later, she had lost her child.

This is of course tragic, but the troubles for all 1,500 deportees had just begun. Once on Mauritius, the deportees were provided with basic accommodation near the harbour. In Madame Elyse's words: "The building we lived in had three floors, each divided into apartments. I think they were built for dock workers. We cleaned the place up, and that was where we lived for fourteen years, until 1987. There were four or five of us in each room."

This shocking episode is an illustration of how we are all pawns to the powers that (there is no other way to look at it) control people's lives. They control where people should live (in the case of the Chagos islanders), and they control what everyone else should know about (in the case of the rest of us).

Significant as these issues may be, I would like to focus on the deposition of these islanders in some makeshift accommodation; this to me shows that people are in some cases treated as nothing more than *commodities*, rather than as human beings. It is simply a case of picking these 'items' up and depositing them in some boxes somewhere else.

This is of course not an isolated example of such behaviour. Isn't this how the ex-British home secretary, Suella Braverman, attempted to solve the asylum seekers conundrum? Let us put these items into little cubicles on an engineless barge in Portland port or, better still, let us put them in an aeroplane and send them to Rwanda. Something similar happened to thousands of people who had emigrated to the US a century ago. They could see the Statue of Liberty as their ship approached the New World, but they were subsequently deposited in tiny tenements which, in time, became the Italian quarter, the Greek or Jewish quarter, etc. Horrendously, this is also how the Jews were treated by the German Nazis. Nothing but insignificant commodities thrown into trains like cattle to be transported to different concentration camps for extermination.

It may not be an exaggeration to say that we approach the provision of housing in this country in a similar way! We say 'we need X number of houses here and Y number of houses there'. House builders then come along and, in most (but not all) cases, they build little cubicles to accommodate families. In every sense these are not *homes*; they are boxes to accommodate items which, for the rest of us, are no longer human beings. We even have National Space standards setting the minimum size for each dwelling type!

Is this what humanity has descended to? Building boxes to house one type of merchandise or other? The situation is much worse when we consider all those people sleeping rough (a few thousand every night) and people who are homeless (around a quarter of a million in the UK).

But let us stay with the question about housing *provision*. The crucial question here is: how do we stop our current practices, and how do we start building homes instead?

Many people have grappled with this question, including the Building Better, Building Beautiful Commission which, in its 2020 report 'Living with Beauty', identified many of the root causes of this malice (merely calling it a problem does not portray the magnitude of the situation). The report concluded that "beauty is not an arbitrary addition to the builder's aims but fundamental to promoting health, well-being and sustainable growth. Beauty is a promise of happiness".

We appear to have nailed it! And yet, we continue to fail! Why?

Is it to do with *ownership*? This cannot be so. Italy, and a number of other Mediterranean countries, have a strong culture of home ownership and yet nobody can claim that Italy's housing position is better than ours.

So, does ownership make a difference? The Margaret Thatcher introduction in the '80s of the Right to Buy encouraged home ownership, but it had disastrous consequences with the loss of a huge number of Council-owned accommodation. That experiment having failed, there must now be justification for empowering councils once again (and further supporting Housing Associations) to build more homes and principally homes which are affordable to those who need them the most. The trouble with this is that councils have now lost the necessary skills and they will need significant funding to be able to do what had once been second nature to them.

Is it to do with *economics*? What most people mean by the housing crisis is middle-class youngsters being unable to save the deposit for a home. We therefore need to make housing more affordable. How can we do that? Probably the only way out now is a commitment to a long-term programme of public investment in public housing, using land that is CPO'd for a cost that is only marginally above current use value. Perhaps we have been deluding ourselves over the last forty years that we can maintain standards without paying for the investment needed and the myth that the private sector can always deliver effective public services.

Is it to do with *building*? It has been repeatedly said that building new homes is highly problematic for the environment. The concrete, bricks, etc, generate large greenhouse gas emissions. Natural materials like timber are in short supply, and we also need trees growing to absorb carbon. Should we therefore focus on renovating and reusing existing housing stock? That surely cannot be enough to cater for our growing population (an increase of around 250,000 people per year).

Is it to do with *politics*? Our politicians carry a lot of responsibility in taking the wrong steps almost at every turn of this miserable saga. "Let's stop the immigrant boats from crossing the Channel," they say, "because immigrants take up housing that our own people require." Or, "Let's build a lot of penthouses for Russian oligarchs and Arab sheikhs," to help the economy. All these are nothing more than distractions from the real issue. None of our politicians in recent years have shown the leadership and daring required to tackle this issue head-on.

Finally, is it to do with *who* builds it? For decades governments have relied on house builders, whose primary objective is to make a profit. Perhaps smaller builders could create neighbourhoods where people live out of choice and not just necessity.

There are many other contributing factors, such as densities (but see how density combined with greed has turned Vauxhall into a grotesque jungle of concrete); location (to build on the green belt or not to build); building materials and methods (see how the Danes have mastered the use of timber); and stewardship (see Charlie Dugdale's pioneering work at Knight Frank). However, it is clear that we have yet to find the silver bullet that might solve the 'housing crisis' in all its ramifications.

Maybe the answer lies in something which is not tangible. Recently, I was struck to read of the case of a sixty-five-year-old lady, Aysen Dennis, who fought against 'gentrification' of the Aylesbury Estate in the London borough of Southwark, where she has lived for thirty years. Unexpectedly, she won, and her words of victory, "they wanted to sell off our community", make it clear that a sense of community is far more important than a renovated house.

In his excellent book *A Home of One's Own*, Hashi Mohamed agrees with this sentiment. He goes on to identify the social, political, economic and many other factors that have resulted in our current predicament of failing to build communities and focusing instead on providing for commodities. In the book he also makes many significant recommendations that would take us a long way towards changing our approach to housing provision. He rightly points out that the issue requires clinical surgery, rather than cosmetics.

What does 'clinical surgery' mean? In my own view, this means that the answer does not lie with economics or ownership, housing numbers or politics. It lies with our *values*. The values of the society that we live in.

This brings to mind Plato's famous utterance about the ideal society which, in his view, will come about if/when politicians become philosophers or conversely if/when philosophers become politicians. The important thing to note here is that Plato's 'politicians' does not carry today's meaning of the word. *Polis* in Greek means 'city', and 'politicians', for Plato, were the citizens!

The answer therefore lies in all of us (the citizens of the world that we live in) becoming philosophers. Easy!

POSTSCRIPT: WILL WE EVER BEGIN TO BUILD HOMES AGAIN?

I asked this question of an old person that I came across one day. You might say that he was a peasant, sitting on a piece of rock, in the middle of nowhere. The sun was blazing in the sky above; the earth was parched; and there was stillness in the air. You could see the veins in his hands; his clothes clung miserably on his skinny body; and his wrinkled face was melancholy. He looked troubled but serene. On hearing my question, he raised his head slowly and wearily to look at me. For a moment, I was rooted to the ground, transfixed by his deep, watery eyes. He did not answer my question himself, but his eyes did. His eyes were like a vast ocean. They told me that there is still humanity in the world and that I shouldn't lose hope.

FRESH BEGINNINGS

Permanence is something that is no longer part of our lives. We live in a turbulent world where everything seems to move fast and is for ever changing. Politics (look how Russia's invasion of Ukraine has affected the lives of everyone in the world), medicine (I need not mention anything other than the Covid vaccine), technology (the internet's impact on our lives has been momentous) and many more…

One of the areas that has undergone a transformation is the way that we work. Gone are the days when people would effectively have a job for life. I understand that nowadays people in the Western world change jobs on average every two years! This is down to many reasons, including personal circumstances, higher expectations, labour mobility and economic upheavals.

It is one of these economic upheavals that forced me to start afresh. I had spent twenty-one very happy years at Colin Buchanan and Partners until that company's acquisition by a large multinational company changed everything. I viewed that acquisition as a great catastrophe for myself and the staff, as well as to the legacy of Sir Colin Buchanan.

However, every setback can also be the launch pad for a new adventure. For example, I have always marvelled at how the defeated Trojans, led by their prince, Aeneas, left Troy burning behind them and set off to rebuild their lives elsewhere, once more. Their journey is brilliantly captured by Virgil in his 'Aeneid' which tells how this dishevelled and bedraggled group of Trojans arrived in Italy and effectively triggered the beginning of the Roman supremacy.

There is no comparison between the two events but, following the acquisition of Colin Buchanan and Partners, I similarly sought pastures new. The corporate world (and the limitations that it placed on my freedom to think) was not for me. As a consequence, I started Markides Associates nearly seven years ago.

So far, the journey has been kind. We now employ thirty-five transport planners and engineers with projects around the UK and Ireland, as well as some work overseas. So, what has this journey taught me so far?

I had not started a business before, nor had I ever thought I would. We are conditioned from an early age to work within a system, to be part of a community. Breaking away from a lifetime's habit is unimaginable, and fear creeps in. That fear stays with you for a long time. Always wondering, *have I done the right thing? Will I be able to make it work? Will people stand by me?*

Aside from the fear, such an enterprise is also revelatory. It is during these times that you find out about people. Those who show care and go out of their way to help, even if it is nothing more than a phone call to check how things are going. On the other hand, there will also be people whose busy lives will have taken them in other directions. Consequently, you find that a whole lifetime's associations become tested, and you therefore need to be prepared to forge new working relationships.

Such an endeavour also brings excitement. You are fighting for survival, and each day is a different challenge. It brings things that are new, unexpected and unforeseen. However, the greatest excitement comes from seeing something being created by your own hands, in front of your own eyes. It is exhilarating!

One of the more significant aspects of this adventure is the freedom it gives you. Suddenly, you realise that there are no rules to follow. You decide on your hours of work, who you should see and work with, which projects to pursue, who to hire and who to let go. The heavy weight of a bureaucratic system is miraculously lifted off your chest, and you can breathe again. It is liberating!

Generating work is a primary preoccupation of any small business. The outcome of that will determine success or failure – and the odds are stacked against you. In many cases, you need to be on frameworks which stipulate dozens of pre-conditions that a small business cannot dream of fulfilling. Some clients will not even consider you because you do not have the prestige of a larger, more established organisation. Others are fearful of your capacity, and even your capabilities, forgetting that you represent many years of experience. You therefore need to be prepared to stand your ground and make a case for yourself.

However, the most important prerequisite is to have a competent and fulfilled group of people around you. Keeping clients happy is essential, and clients are kept happy by good work.

But what generates good work? In my view, a *happy* workforce is a fundamental requirement. Nothing can beat a happy office! Consequently, making friendships at work is what will give rise to good work and hence success.

Finally, a fundamental requirement for anyone starting a small business is family support. People who not only believe in you but are prepared to bolster your confidence when those dark days of rejection and doubt arrive. There will inevitably be days when you feel you should throw in the towel. That is when you need that one person at home to remind you of who you are and what you are capable of.

Starting a new business requires a lot of energy and mental fortitude, but it is also rich in experiences and emotions.

ANTIGONE

All my life I have carried this one word – 'duty' – on my shoulders like Atlas carries the whole world on his shoulders! That duty has manifested itself in many forms – duty towards myself, my family, the people I work with and even my country. This one word has been accompanying me and all the time spurring me to ask the question: am I upholding moral principles, and am I doing the very best that I can? The following example should suffice in explaining what I mean.

When I was doing my national service in the Cyprus army, there was one soldier who was a bully. He did not need to terrorise everyone in our dormitory, but he did – particularly one or two of the weaker characters. One day he was again belittling someone when I intervened. I did not have to, and it would have been much safer if I had stayed out of it, but my sense of duty made me step forward in defence of that other soldier. This inevitably led to what turned out to be a very fierce brawl with the bully. We were like two wild animals throwing punches, kicking and biting each other ferociously. At one point we both stood up in the middle of the dormitory and, shaking from the physical exertion, blood on our faces, we looked at each other. That was it! With all the other soldiers watching in a circle around us, we both turned away, and we all knew that that would be the end of his bullying.

The question is: why did I do it? I could very easily have stayed out of it. I knew perfectly that my interference would mean trouble for me, and yet, something inside me made me step forward. That sense of restoring fair play amongst the dormitory was nothing but instinct, and it was that instinct that dictated my duty.

What *is* duty? Is duty an inner voice that tells each one of us what we should do as we take different steps in our life? Or is it simply doing our job? The latter explanation is the reason given by several Nazis for their different crimes during the Second World War. At the Nuremberg trial they defended themselves by saying that they were simply obeying orders and carrying out their duties; whatever happened was therefore not their fault!

What about all of us in the built environment profession? On a daily basis, do we carry out our duty? Is that our duty towards our employer? Is it our duty towards the client? And what if we do not agree with the client? What if the client wants to build a monstrosity because that is what will make him the most money? Do we still have a duty towards him/her? What about the duty to ourselves?

Thousands of young men died in the trenches of the First World War carrying out their duty towards their country; it was by all accounts a slaughter, and yet only a few of them questioned their orders. The vast majority of them simply got on with their proclaimed duty, even though they knew that most likely they would be killed. Were they doing so because they were following orders or because of the sense of duty towards their country (or maybe both)?

What about the famous case of Muhammad Ali who refused to go to fight in Vietnam like so many other young Americans in the 1960s? Was he failing to do his duty towards his country, or was he following his inner voice and therefore doing his duty towards his conscience? I have often wondered what my position would be in similar circumstances. Would I have had the courage to say *no* to Tony Blair, or would I have followed all the thousands of British soldiers who went and fought in Iraq on the basis of a 'dodgy dossier'?

Dodgy or not, some people might claim that it is our duty to fight if so required by our country. In fact, even Socrates seems to agree with this. Following his sentence to death (on very dubious grounds), and a day before he was due to take poison in prison, his influential followers came to see him. They had important news to tell him as they had bribed the guards and commissioned a ship that would take him to Sicily where he could live the rest of his life in freedom. His response was startling: "The court has sentenced me to death; it is my duty to follow the laws of my country!"

I do not often disagree with Socrates, but in this case I think that I do – I would have taken the ship to Sicily, especially as I knew that my sentencing was on fabricated grounds! Does this mean that I have no loyalty to the laws of my country? Or, even worse, am I as bad as Gyges as described by Herodotus in one of his most famous anecdotes? That story goes like this:

Gyges was a young shepherd in Lydia, Mesopotamia. When out with his flock one day, he found a ring in a cave. Some days later, he noticed that, by twisting the ring on his finger, he disappeared. Those around him began speaking of him as if he was not there. Having acquired this new ability to become invisible, Gyges used his magic ring to gain the graces of the queen, who he seduced. With the power to go undetected, he then managed to conspire with the queen to kill the king and take over the kingdom. What is the moral of this story? Gyges would assert that people behave in a morally acceptable way *only* as a result of the fear of being caught. Gyges goes on to say that, if we had the power of doing wrong with impunity (i.e. if we had his magic ring to become invisible), we would, like him, do everything possible to advance our own interests. In other words, people do not behave as a result of a sense of duty towards the others.

So, are we humans *by nature* selfish and without any sense of responsibility? Do we obey the laws of our country/workplace/community because it is convenient to do so and because they make our life easier? What about my sense of duty towards my fellow soldier in the example given above? That was not following any laws; in fact, I might have got into trouble with the laws of the military if the brawl had got to the ears of our officers!

The answer to these conflicting points is given (for me at least) by Sophocles in his famous play *Antigone*. In that play, the king of Thebes gives orders that Antigone's brother should not be buried because he was a traitor to their city. Yet Antigone defies the king's orders, and she secretly buries her brother. The play is all about Antigone versus the king. Youth against the old. Woman against man but, above all, it is about the duty to ourselves as opposed to the duty towards the king. Why does Antigone do what she does? She does it because it is her duty to bury her brother and because (as she very bravely asserts in front of the king) there are the *human laws* which take precedence over his own laws. In other words, it is her conscience that tells her what is right and what is wrong – and it is that conscience that defines her duty.

It seems to me that in the final analysis, it comes down to our human values (or conscience, if you like). The question is: are my values and sense of duty the same as the next person's? I know they *should* be, but are they? And if they are not, does that then mean that we need a set of parameters (let's call them the laws of the country) that define how we should all behave in a civilised society? If it comes down to laws, does it mean that Antigone was wrong to defy the king and that (yet again) Socrates was correct?

HADES

One of the most beautiful passages in Homer is the encounter between Odysseus and Achilles, in the underworld. When alive, Achilles had sought nothing but glory. He was the fastest, the bravest and most fearless of all warriors with just one motivation: for his name to be remembered for ever. He did not wish to be like all the others; like those millions and billions of people who pass this earth without making a mark. He wanted to stand out!

And yet, when prompted by Odysseus in the underworld, Achilles tells Odysseus that it is terrible to be a shade in the land of the dead. Even a revered ghost like himself finds no solace in his fame. He knows that it is too late now, but he readily and sorrowfully admits that it is better to be a nobody, even a landless peasant, in the land of the living than a famous hero among the dead.

I remembered this story when thinking about my own life. In particular, at sixty-three, I know that I have already travelled more than three quarters of my likely journey on this earth. Hades is just round the corner!

This, therefore, is a moment of reflection. What have I achieved in life? Has my life been worth it? What was my existence for? And the most alarming question of all: have I led a *good life*?

Let's take each one of these questions in turn. What have I achieved in life? Every time I consider this question, I think about so many other people's 'body of work' – whether in commerce, the built environment, literature, sport or any other aspect of life. Compared to many of these people, what body of work have I produced? Doesn't my body of work at Colin Buchanan and subsequently at Markides Associates pale into insignificance when compared to such people?

Despite my meagre contribution to the world, has my life been worth it? I hope that the answer is *yes*. My children in particular are by far my greatest pride as, through them, I know that I will have contributed to a better world.

This takes us to the bigger question: what has my existence been for? Was there a purpose to it, or are we all just 'ships passing in the night'? Certainly, I have not written a *War and Peace* like Tolstoy, nor have I marked history like Alexander the Great, Julius Caesar or Churchill. I have not even written a simple jingle of a song that would have been enjoyed by millions (or even just a few dozen) people. Does this mean that my life has been meaningless? I refuse to accept this. There *must* be a reason for my existence. But then, what is it?

In answer to this, I am reminded of a short discussion I had with a monk when I visited Mount Athos, in Greece, a few years ago. I was with a group of friends, and we asked the monk to tell us what we should be teaching our children in order that they may grow up into good human beings. His reply astounded me.

"Never tell them what to do. Just show them on a daily basis, by the way you conduct your own lives!"

So, the answer to my question about the reason for my existence probably does not lie in 'grand gestures'. It is not necessary to produce Shakespeare's body of work or to have written Beethoven's Symphony No. 9 or to have conquered the whole of Asia like Cyrus the Great and his Persian empire.

It is enough to have lived our lives quietly, as it is the *little gestures* that influence the people around us and therefore help to shape the world. This must be right, because what I remember from my childhood is the blossom of the orchards in the spring; the overpowering scent that came from my mother's basil plants every evening when she systematically went about watering them; the crackling sound whenever I dug a knife into a watermelon and opened it to reveal the stunning red flesh inside; and the pain I felt in my heart when one day, many years ago, I saw a boy squash a sparrow to death by stamping on it.

The same principle applies to my professional life. Isn't it strange that, in nearly forty years of working, one moment that stands out was when I had finished reciting a poem to a group of engineers? At the end, one of them approached me and said, "I loved that poem! When I go home, I will seek out that poet and read some more." Little gestures and moments such as this are what make our lives meaningful. This *must* be the reason that we exist.

And this takes me to the last holiday that I enjoyed with my wife. I can still clearly see us walking on a beach under a grey sky whilst trying in vain to protect ourselves against the strong wind. Our dog was running around us, wet from the waves and as exhilarated as we were in that moment. I knew that these moments would later be recounted to and shared with our family and friends. Isn't this my contribution to the world, and isn't this the reason for my existence? In a tiny way, I have knitted together (just like the black-clad women sitting on their doorstep in Cyprus endlessly knit their famous laces) the whole world!

And I now move on to the most alarming question of all: have I led a good life? I have always jokingly said that I would give anything in order to have a dialogue (about any subject) with the philosopher Socrates! I want to give him the opportunity to question me (just like he did with his contemporary Athenians) about my life. I want him to put me to the test – am I leading a 'good life', and if not, how can I change in order that I *will* lead a good life, as that is what I have always wanted?

Well, very soon I will get my chance as I too will become nothing but a ghost in the underworld – amongst Socrates, Achilles and billions of others. There, in Hades,

I will be able to search Socrates out, and the two of us can then have the dialogue that, all my life, I have so much longed for! He should be able to help me answer this question.

Just before that, when the ferryman arrives to take me across the River Styx, I will make sure to give him a valueless coin – a very small gesture, similar to all the other little gestures and contributions that have made up my life.

A FEW WORDS ABOUT THE AUTHOR

Andreas Markides is a chartered civil engineer with a masters in transport planning from Imperial College. In the past, he had been Chairman of Colin Buchanan and Partners. He is the founder of Markides Associates, a consultancy which employs thirty-five engineers and transport planners.

Andreas was President of the Chartered Institution of Highways and Transportation (CIHT) during 2017/18 and is currently the chair of the Academy of Urbanism.

Andreas grew up in Cyprus and came to England in the late 70s as a refugee, following the invasion of Cyprus by Turkey. For the last forty years, he has lived in Hampshire with his wife Kay and their four children. He is an advocate of sustainable transport and is passionate about the creation of better and liveable places.

www.ingramcontent.com/pod-product-compliance
Lightning Source LLC
Chambersburg PA
CBHW060749240726
48664CB00009BA/1673